WONDERS OF MAN

THE COLOSSEUM

by Peter Quennell

and the Editors
of the Newsweek Book Division

NEWSWEEK, New York

NEWSWEEK BOOK DIVISION

JOSEPH L. GARDNER   *Editor*

Edwin D. Bayrd, Jr.   *Associate Editor*
Laurie P. Phillips   *Picture Editor*
Eva Galan   *Assistant Editor*
Lynne H. Brown   *Copy Editor*
Russell Ash   *European Correspondent*

S. ARTHUR DEMBNER   *Publisher*

WONDERS OF MAN

MILTON GENDEL   *Consulting Editor*

Contents

Introduction

For nineteen centuries the Colosseum has stood as the hulking, awesome symbol of the Eternal City. The giant ellipse, enclosed by its dramatically repetitious tiers of arches, creates a unique visual impact, one that stimulated the creative talents of poets and painters from Goethe and Lord Byron to George Bernard Shaw, from Bruegel to Turner. Rome's memorable attraction can surely lay claim to the title of history's most famous monument.

The people of ancient Rome, the eloquent author of the following narrative reminds us, were kept satisfied with a nearly endless succession of entertainments such as gladiatorial games and wild beast hunts. And for this purpose, in the first century A.D., Vespasian and his two sons and successors — the Flavian emperors — built the Colosseum. More accurately known as the Flavian Amphitheater, the arena also witnessed harrowing scenes of Christian martyrdom, and it is to those martyrs that the edifice is now dedicated.

To the generations of tourists who have come to gaze in admiration and wonder, the vast arena has long appeared ageless — always ancient, always silent, always crumbling and ruinous. It is difficult to imagine it as it must have been when new: with sunlight striking its unblemished surfaces and flashing off the statues that decorated the arches; with hordes of people in a holiday mood dwarfed by its bulk as they approached across a broad plaza; and inside, with ring after ring of excited spectators cheering the bloody spectacles being presented for their amusement.

The last gladiatorial games were held in the Colosseum in 404, and only occasionally since then — for such incongruous events as a bullfight, weekly sermons, and a Verdi concert — has it been publicly used. During succeeding centuries, the damage caused by earthquakes was more than matched by the heedless plundering of Roman citizens who used it as a convenient quarry. Incredibly, only in the last two centuries was thought given to preservation of the structure — then in danger of complete collapse. Today, unfortunately, the wondrous ruin has a new enemy: the automobile, which with its noise and fumes surrounds and isolates the arena. But it is the automobile, or more precisely the commodious tour bus, that now brings an ever-increasing stream of tourists, visitors who can happily report back home that the Colosseum indeed still stands and thus — according to the hallowed aphorism — Rome and the world as well.

THE EDITORS

THE STORY
OF THE COLOSSEUM

I

ROMA RESURGENS

Nero's Golden House, a huge complex of lofty, fantastic structures that spanned the valley between the Palatine and Esquiline hills, was the largest, strangest, and most grandiose palace yet built by any Roman emperor. Once it had taken shape, Nero expressed his joy; at last, he said, he could begin to live like a decent human being! The Golden House satisfied both his passionate love of luxury and his fastidious sense of style. In the entrance hall stood a statue of the owner some 120 feet high; and its many dining rooms were roofed with ivory panels, which slid back to release a rain of scent or discharge a cascade of freshly gathered roses. The palace, we learn, enclosed an enormous pool, "surrounded by buildings made to resemble cities," and a garden, extensive as a miniature park, where many kinds of animals, wild and tame, wandered freely amid lawns and bowers.

The Emperor Nero, last of the Julio-Claudian line that stretched back to Julius Caesar, was above all else an aesthete, and he was much more concerned with his achievements as an artist than with his functions as a head of state. Nevertheless, he chose his officers shrewdly — among them Titus Flavius Vespasianus, that capable soldier whom he had ordered to reconquer Palestine. And despite the emperor's private eccentricities, the vast extent of the Roman Empire was particularly well-administered during his fourteen-year reign, from A.D. 54 to 68. Seen through Roman eyes, his greatest offense, perhaps, was not his extravagance or his cruelty but his wild artistic vanity, which he indulged by appearing on the stage as a singer and an actor, often wearing an unbelted silken robe. Offensive, too, was the preference he showed for the company of his Greek and Eastern subjects. Only a Greek audience, he declared, knew how to listen to music; the Greeks alone were really worthy of his genius. On one occasion, when he was urgently needed at Rome, he refused again and again to leave Greece until he had concluded his latest concert tour and had fully proved that he deserved his fame.

Thus news of the military revolts abroad that broke out early in the year 68 did not at first affect the emperor's spirits. "On the contrary," writes his biographer, the second-century historian Suetonius, "he celebrated whatever good news came . . . with the most lavish banquets imaginable, and composed comic songs about the leaders of the revolt, which he set to bawdy tunes and sang with appropriate gestures. . . ." Those songs, Suetonius adds, soon caught the fancy of the public and were sung long after the composer's death. Nero's belief in his literary and musical gifts was not entirely unfounded. Even Suetonius, who did all that he could to blacken the emperor's reputation and to draw an improving contrast between the excesses of the Julio-Claudians and the virtues of the Antonine dynasty under which he lived and wrote, is obliged to admit that Nero had some original poetic talents and "took more than an amateur's interest" in painting and sculpture and the other arts he did not practice.

While the insurrection was confined to the provinces, the emperor's mood remained cheerful. Then, during the hours of darkness, enemies began plastering his statues with roughly scribbled threats and insults. Dispatches from Spain and Gaul grew more and more alarming, and one night Nero awoke at midnight — for the last few days, he had been vexed by terrible dreams — to find his palace almost empty. His guests had quietly packed up and departed. Gone, too, were his guards and household servants. Regaining his bedroom, which he had left in order to search for help, Nero discovered that his valets had already made away not only with his bed coverings but with a precious box of lethal drugs, which his favorite poisoner, Locusta, had prepared against emergencies.

It was now merely a question of deciding how and where he ought to meet his death. He shouted for the gladiator Spiculus, an experienced swordsman who might have killed him at a single blow, but Spiculus had joined the fugitives. Next, he thought of drowning in the Tiber but immediately changed his mind. What he needed, he said, was a period of rest and reflection. An imperial freedman named Phaon, one of the handful of devoted attendants who presently rallied around their sovereign, offered Nero a temporary refuge in his own secluded villa, which stood at a convenient distance just beyond the city. Nero agreed and, escorted by four companions including his beloved Sporus, rode out into the hostile streets. He was wearing an old hat and a tattered cloak, and across his face he held a handkerchief. The party cleared the city, but Nero was alarmed by the uproar from a neighboring military camp, a slight earthquake tremor that shook the ground, and a pallid sheet of summer lightning. Moreover, his horse shied at the stench of a dead body that happened to be lying near the road, and as he dropped the handkerchief that concealed his face, a passing veteran recognized the emperor and automatically saluted him.

They were now approaching the villa, and Nero's panic fears increased. But when Phaon begged him to hide in a gravel pit he retorted, with a flash of his old arrogance, that he refused to go underground before he died. Because it seemed dangerous to open the main gates, his servants scraped a hole beneath the wall; and the stout emperor, having somehow scrambled through, took refuge in a slave's cubicle, where he collapsed upon a wretched mattress. Rather than face capture, his companions suggested that he should make a Roman end. He assented miserably and bade them dig a grave. Yet, even then, as he watched them delve and shovel, he continued to brood about his wasted genius. *"Qualis artifex pereo!"* he exclaimed. "What an artist perishes in me!"

He might have continued to brood and hesitate had not an ominous message arrived from Rome. The Senate had voted him a public enemy and had decreed that he was to be punished "in the ancient style" — which meant, his attendants explained, that with his head in a wooden fork he would be slowly flogged to death. It was his personal cowardice and the indignity of his present position, after a life so promising and well-spent, that apparently caused Nero the most dismay. "How ugly and vulgar my life has become!" he sighed; and in Greek, the language he had always loved, "This does Nero no credit." Finally, the sound of a troop of cavalry, clattering down the lane toward the villa, roused him from his gloomy trance. Assisted by his secretary, Epaphroditus, he raised a dagger to his throat and dealt himself a mortal blow.

Nero died at the age of thirty-one. He was a gross young man, paunchy and spindle-legged, with a bull neck, light blond hair crimped in the fashion affected by his favorite associates, the Roman charioteers, and a reddish-golden beard (which he had inherited from his father's family, the Ahenobarbi, or bronze-bearded) curling around his heavy cheeks. Although most Ro-

mans rejoiced to hear of his end, and "citizens ran through the streets wearing caps of liberty," the dead man did not lack supporters. No one attempted to dishonor Nero's remains, and he was carried to the funeral pyre wearing gold-embroidered robes. The ceremony, we learn from Suetonius, cost two thousand gold pieces; and for some years, every spring and summer, a group of unknown friends persisted in bringing garlands of flowers to his dignified tomb upon the Pincian Hill.

Nor were Nero's achievements as a ruler completely forgotten. The Emperor Trajan praised his splendid reconstruction of Rome after the great fire of 64, a catastrophe that some of his critics declared he had himself arranged; while Vitellius, the last of three emperors who briefly succeeded him during the years 68 and 69, was accustomed to applaud his skill in music. "Now sing one of the Master's songs," he would say. As a modern historian remarks, no compliment would have pleased Nero more.

Later sovereigns were not so respectful of Nero's accomplishments and showed little regard for his most ambitious construction, the Golden House. And today on the site of the *stagnum*, or lake, that once beautified the gardens of that splendid edifice, stands the Colosseum. This was the masterpiece of Vespasian, the soldier who had served Nero in Africa and Palestine, a very different personage whose character was as cautious and shrewd and orderly as his predecessor's had been rash and wild.

Vespasian did not snatch at authority; he mounted to power by carefully measured steps. Nero's sudden extinction had plunged the empire into eighteen months of civil war, and during those months, Galba, Otho, and

Vitellius had each assumed the purple and had each met a violent end: Galba murdered by his soldiers; Otho driven to commit suicide; Vitellius, probably the worst of the trio, slaughtered in a public street. Meanwhile Vespasian was quietly moving toward Rome from Palestine, whither Nero had dispatched him to subdue the Jewish rebels. He was sixty years old, and nothing about his past career hinted at his future greatness.

True, he had fought well in Germany and Britain, where he had subjugated two hostile tribes and conquered the whole Isle of Wight, and had become a trusted servant of the empire. But he had gravely offended Nero on one of his musical tours, either by leaving the room while the emperor was singing or — Suetonius gives both versions of the story — by remaining and falling fast asleep. When disgrace followed, Vespasian had fled for his life; he remained in exile until Nero decided to relent and again gave him a high command.

This terrifying experience had made Vespasian more than ever wary, and despite the death of Nero and the outbreak of civil war in Rome, he still hesitated to quit his distant province. But, like most Romans, he was a great believer in oracles; and among the oracles Vespasian consulted was that of the Jewish Yahweh, whom Suetonius calls "the God of Carmel." The oracle promised that, however exalted the aim he had set himself, he would not be disappointed in his plans. Mysterious omens helped to encourage him: the appearance of an ox that burst into his dining room and fell at his feet "as if suddenly exhausted," and of a stray dog that had picked up a human hand — a hand being an emblem of power — and dropped it underneath his breakfast table.

Clearly, the gods must intend that Vespasian should rule. Moving on to Egypt from Palestine, he was proclaimed emperor at Alexandria. There, too, he consulted a local divinity; entering the temple of Serapis to discover how long he was destined to reign, he was granted an extremely hopeful vision. Serapis indicated, moreover, that Vespasian now possessed the gift of healing, at which point he is said to have worked two minor miracles. Simultaneously, a coven of Greek soothsayers was inspired to excavate a sacred site, where they turned up a hoard of ancient vessels — all of them painted with Vespasian's portrait.

The new emperor finally reached Rome toward the end of 69. He found a gigantic task confronting him, for Nero and his three immediate successors had almost drained the Roman treasury. Nero alone, who was prepared to spend the equivalent of $84,000 on the roses he imported from Egypt for a single private banquet, had run through $42,500,000; and his example had been followed by Vitellius, whose private tastes were scarcely less expensive.

Vespasian's first concern was to solve the budgetary problem, which he attacked like a modern accountant called in to save a bankrupt firm. He calculated that, to pay off the government's debts, he needed 40 billion gold pieces; and not all the measures he adopted were either popular or scrupulous. Thus Vespasian revived taxes that earlier emperors had abolished or invented new exactions, sold public offices to the highest bidder, and sometimes himself engaged in dubious financial dealings "such as cornering the stocks of certain commodities and then putting them back on the market at inflated prices." But very little of the money he raised went into Vespasian's own pocket. The life he led was conspicuously modest and frugal, and Nero's old friends often described him as a vulgar money-grabbing boor.

Yet no Roman emperor could afford to be altogether parsimonious; and it was by alternating parsimony with generosity that Vespasian established his imperial position. Besides subsidizing needy senators and impoverished former consuls, he distributed large rewards among musicians and actors and held lavish public dinner parties. At the same time, he began rebuilding Rome. Many Roman rulers employed the coinage to advertise their great achievements; and Vespasian's coins carried the proud legend *Roma resurgens* — Rome arising from its ashes.

During the civil war, the Capitol had been burned down. Vespasian inaugurated its clearing and restoration, shouldering the first basketful of broken masonry himself. He also started work on several splendid new buildings: a Temple of Peace near the Forum; a sanctuary dedicated to the Divine Claudius, Nero's ill-fated stepfather; and the Colosseum, or Flavian Amphitheater. Destined to become the most famous monument of ancient Rome, the Colosseum was begun in the year 72 and was still uncompleted at the time of Vespasian's death seven years later.

Physically, Vespasian himself bore a certain resemblance to the Colosseum — large, plain, and immensely solid, with few pretensions to superficial elegance. The Julio-Claudians were an aristocratic line — nervous, extravagant, and inbred. Vespasian, founder of the Flavian dynasty, belonged to the official upper-middle class. He came of a family of soldiers and civil servants, his grandfather having been a centurion who fought under Pompey against Julius Caesar but then obtained an honorable discharge and took to the lucrative business of tax collecting. Vespasian's father, Sabinus, had been a tax collector in Asia, where he had earned a reputation for unusual honesty. Vespasian, the younger of Sabinus's two sons, was born on November 17, A.D. 7, at the village of Falacrina just beyond Reiti, among the pleasant Sabine Hills.

Vespasian was passionately devoted to the scenes of his youth; at heart, he remained a sober countryman. His paternal grandmother, Tertulla, had reared the boy upon her farm, and after he had become emperor, according to Suetonius, he frequently revisited the old house, which he kept exactly as it had been in his boyhood. On feast days he made a habit of drinking from the little silver cup that his grandmother had once used.

Both the coin he struck to commemorate his conquest of the Jews and a surviving marble bust have immortalized Vespasian's rugged features. The neck is thick, the jaw is boldly prominent, the forehead and jowl are deeply wrinkled, and the nose is large and decisive. He often smiled, writes Suetonius, yet "always wore a strained expression." Otherwise, he was strong and square-shouldered and enjoyed admirable health, although — apart from having himself regularly massaged and fasting one day every month — he did nothing to preserve it.

His habits were simple. He would rise punctually, sometimes before dawn, and read reports and private letters. Then, while he dressed and put on his shoes, his friends would bid him good morning. And once the most urgent affairs of the day had been settled, he would take a short drive. From this excursion he returned for a siesta with one of the several mistresses who

entertained him in his later years. Finally, he entered
the bath, and later he proceeded to his dining room.
At dinner his mood was invariably cheerful, and it was
then that his attendants asked any special favors of him.

Vespasian was a good-humored man who never harbored old grudges. Much earlier, when he had been
expelled from Nero's court and had asked an imperial
chamberlain where he should go, the courtier pushed
him out of the palace, roughly recommending that he
go to hell. After Vespasian's accession, the official begged
for forgiveness; the emperor merely showed him the
door, repeating just the same words. Such leniency surprised and delighted his subjects, who remembered the
savage record of the Julio-Claudian emperors. Unlike
them, Vespasian was neither a sadist nor a cultivated
debauchee. Though by no means a puritan himself, he
mistrusted the luxurious excesses of the fashionable
Roman world. He had persuaded the Senate to ordain
that any free woman who took a slave as a lover should
be reduced to servile status. Effeminacy also shocked
him. A smart young officer, reeking of scent, who arrived
to thank the emperor for promotion, was brusquely sent
about his business. Vespasian canceled the promotion,
remarking that he would have been far less displeased
had the fellow smelled of honest garlic.

During his lifetime, Vespasian's jokes were famous —
pithy, incisive, seldom delicate, and often made at the
expense of his own bizarre financial dealings. One of his
most ingenious schemes was to levy a tax on the produce
of the city's public urinals, which he learned had a considerable value for the Roman guild of fullers. (The
fullers were the dry cleaners of Rome. They had discovered that the ammonia in urine had certain valuable

cleansing properties.) His son Titus, a much more sensitive person, protested indignantly against the new tax.
But pushing a coin beneath his son's nose, Vespasian
reminded him, in one of his best-known phrases, that
gold has no unpleasant odor.

Until he died, the emperor continued to joke; and his
last joke was perhaps his best. While he was visiting
southern Italy in the late spring or early summer of 79,
Vespasian came down with a dangerous fever and hurried back toward the capital, then to his grandmother's
old house at Reiti. There he caught a chill and was
obliged to go to bed, although he continued to receive
deputations and to transact official business. But before
long he felt his strength declining.

On his death, every respectable emperor was pro-
moted to divine rank; and Vespasian, who had always
interpreted his role in the most worldly and prosaic
fashion, could not help being amused by the idea that
he would very soon be deified. *"Vae, puto, deus fio,"* he
exclaimed. "My word! I think I must be becoming a
god." Not long afterward he suffered a violent seizure,
nearly fainted, but — crying that an emperor should
die on his feet — made a last desperate effort to rise,
only to fall dead into his attendants' arms. The date
was June 23, 79. Seven years younger than the century,
he had reigned a whole decade.

Vespasian was succeeded by his elder son, Titus; and
it was Titus who undertook the completion of the Flavian Amphitheater, which his father had begun to raise
in 72. At his accession, the second ruler of the Flavian
line was a man of nearly forty; and like Vespasian, he
had served with distinction both in Germany and in
Britain. Left behind in Judaea when his father moved

to Rome, Titus had carried on the offensive against the Jewish rebels. At the head of a legion, he had captured two important fortified cities and singlehanded had killed a dozen of the enemy, being careful not to waste an arrow.

Vespasian had already subdued the district south of Jerusalem; and in the year 70, Titus laid siege to the city itself. The historian Tacitus, who deeply detested the Jews — "among the Jews [he noted] all things are profane that we hold sacred" — describes the tremendous fortifications of ancient Jerusalem as they looked down upon the Roman army:

> The city occupied a commanding position, and it had been reinforced by engineering works so massive that they might have rendered even a flat site impregnable. Two lofty hills were enclosed by walls skilfully staggered and forming re-entrant angles designed to expose the flank of an attacker. At the edge of the crags was a sharp drop, and a series of towers dominated the scene, sixty feet high where the rising ground helped, and one hundred and twenty feet high in the hollows between.

During the siege, Tacitus continues, numerous prodigies occurred:

> In the sky appeared a vision of armies in conflict, of glittering armour. A sudden lightning flash . . . lit up the Temple. The doors of the holy place abruptly opened, a superhuman voice was heard to declare that the gods were leaving it, and in the same instant came the rushing tumult of their departure.

Any people except the Jews, remarks Tacitus, would have immediately offered solemn sacrifices. They, on the other hand, took comfort from "the ancient scriptures of their priests," believing that the time had now come when the East would triumph and "from Judaea would go men destined to rule the world." These prophesies, Tacitus explains, really referred to the victory of Vespasian and Titus. Despite the fierce courage that the inhabitants of Jerusalem displayed, Titus eventually breached their walls and, on August 10, broke through the defenses of the Temple. Its Mosaic treasures were carried away and the buildings burned down. Prisoners were massacred or thrown to wild beasts while the sacrilegious eagle standard of Rome was planted in the Hebrew Holy of Holies.

The fortress of Masada had yet to be overcome — it did not fall for another three years, when its entire garrison of Zealot fanatics simultaneously committed suicide. But with the fall of Jerusalem, Jewish resistance as a whole had come to an end and the province of Judaea, after three years of patriotic struggle, was safely reintegrated into the Roman Empire.

The Romans' attitude toward the Jews may be compared with their attitude toward the Christians. Both sorely tried the imperial government's patience. It was not their religious beliefs that aroused hostility; the empire had always been full of strange religions. What caused alarm was the astonishing doggedness with which they defended their peculiar faiths and the effect of those faiths on their political and social outlook.

No Roman conqueror was expected to be merciful and Titus was no exception. He utterly destroyed Jerusalem. He also did his best to extirpate the Jewish faith, which, he rightly assumed, had been the keystone of the nation's long resistance. The arch that was afterward raised to his memory, at the end of the Sacred Way not far from the Colosseum, is decorated with a relief that shows the treasures of the Temple — among them the Mosaic seven-branched candelabra — being carried in his Roman triumph.

Although Titus was the hammer of the Jews, he proved a kindly sovereign to his own people. This surprised his subjects. As a young man, he had acquired a reputation for cruelty and profligacy. He was said to have murdered the ex-consul Aulus Caecina and other important Roman citizens; and there was talk of "riotous parties which he kept going with his more extravagant friends far into the night." He was also rumored to maintain "a troop of inverts and eunuchs." His guilty passion for Queen Berenice, daughter of the Jewish monarch Herod Agrippa, "to whom he had allegedly promised marriage," had provided his critics with a further source of scandal.

These stories may well have been baseless, for Suetonius, lacking more accurate forms of evidence, was often obliged to rely on popular legend and remembered gossip. Certainly, once he had succeeded Vespasian, Titus revealed a very different character. He was notably generous, respected private property, and his dinner parties, "far from being orgies, were very pleasant occasions," attended by his most respectable subjects. Queen Berenice he dismissed from Rome, though the separation hurt them both. He "broke off relations with some of his favorite boys," and when they made a name for themselves on the stage, he never attended their performances. Informers, the scourge of Roman society, the emperor ordered to be severely beaten. At gladiatorial shows in the brand-new Colosseum, Titus would noisily argue with the crowd, and now and then he would frequent the public baths, so as to be able to meet even the humblest citizens of the city.

Thus Titus was generally loved and respected. His personal appearance, too, was prepossessing. His busts show a rather plump face, small eyes, a fleshy hook nose, and a swelling double chin. But Suetonius, who speaks of the emperor's "beauty," asserts that he was graceful, dignified, muscular, and handsome, and that apart from a certain stoutness, he had no apparent flaws. With good looks he combined a keen intelligence. He had an admirable memory, wrote verse and speeches in Latin and Greek, or improvised them as he went along. He had mastered shorthand and could imitate any script, claiming that, had he not been an emperor, he would have been a brilliant forger. Incidentally, he was also an amateur musician who sang agreeably and had learned to play the harp.

Titus's reign, however, was darkened by a succession of catastrophes. Vesuvius erupted, burying Pompeii as well as the neighboring cities of Stabiae and Herculaneum; there was a terrible outbreak of plague, one of the worst that had yet attacked the empire; and a fire, which burned for three days and three nights, swept through the crowded streets of Rome. The emperor's concern, Suetonius writes, was that of a parent for his injured children. He set up a board to relieve distress in the south, endeavored to check the onset of the plague by organizing both medical help and every kind of propitiatory sacrifice, and in order to restore the damage caused by the great fire, stripped the decorations from his own houses.

Unhappily, the reign of Titus was brief. At the end of the games in August 81 he was observed to shed tears. He felt gloomy forebodings. A sacrificial victim had

broken away when he was about to administer the death blow, and thunder had rolled from an unclouded heaven. Like Vespasian, he decided to seek refuge in his family's homestead among the Sabine Hills. But at the first stage of his journey, he developed a dangerous fever. And as he continued on, he is said to have drawn back the curtain of his litter, lifted his head toward the summer sky, and complained that he did not deserve his fate, since — to the best of his recollection — he had but a single crime on his conscience.

What that crime was the historian could not tell, though at the time there were some who imagined that Titus was referring to an illicit relationship (which she herself always strenuously denied) with his brother's wife, Domitia. It has also been suggested that the offense he had in mind was his profanation of the Hebrew Holy of Holies — a god was still a god, even if worshiped by a hostile people, and the vanquished Jews apparently attributed his death to this rash act of impiety. Had he lived, the generous and scrupulous emperor might perhaps have made amends. As it was, he died, like Vespasian, soon after reaching the old family house, on September 13, 81, having reigned for twenty-six months and twenty days.

In a young man's life, neither a famous father nor an exceptionally virtuous brother may turn out to be an unmixed blessing. Domitian had long been overshadowed, first by his father, Vespasian, then by his brother, Titus, and his attempts to prove his own worth very rarely proved successful. He was often snubbed and reprimanded. When Vespasian and Titus headed a procession, seated on their chariots or curule chairs, Domitian humbly rode behind them. He affected a modest air and pretended to be more interested in poetry than in politics and statesmanship. But once Titus occupied their father's throne, Domitian rapidly showed his hand as a jealous and vindictive rival.

At his accession, Domitian was twenty-nine, and his brother's death had caught him unprepared. He had a solitary nature; and at the beginning of his fifteen-year reign, writes Suetonius, he would sit alone hour after hour, catching flies and neatly killing them with a needle-sharp pen. For his wife, Domitia, whom he was obliged to divorce when she became enamored of the fashionable actor Paris, he clearly felt a real affection; and he invented a lame pretext to call Domitia back when he discovered that he missed her company. Suetonius believed that Domitian had not been naturally evil, so much as immature and ill-adjusted. He needed friends, and in the terrible solitude that surrounds an absolute monarch, genuine friends are always hard to come by. Hence, Domitian's curious choice of confidants. At every gladiatorial show he attended, we learn, he would talk, "sometimes in very serious tone," to a little boy with a grotesquely small skull who always stood beside him dressed in red. "Can you guess why I have just appointed Mettius Rufus Prefect of Egypt?" he was once overheard to ask the child.

Domitian had none of his brother's self-conscious rectitude. Indeed, there was something almost Hamlet-like about his neurotic moods and his sudden bursts of cruelty. At first, his virtues had held his vices in check; later, Suetonius records, he "transformed his virtues into vices." Meanwhile, having adopted the titles *Dominus et Deus,* Lord and God, he did his best to play his imperial part with appropriate grace and dignity. In the

new Colosseum, which was opened during his brother's reign but which Domitian completed, he held particularly lavish shows. He was also responsible for instituting a festival of music, gymnastics, and horsemanship over which he himself presided wearing a golden diadem and a purple Greek robe. Simultaneously, Domitian patronized literature and organized competitions, with splendid prizes, between contemporary poets and musicians. To the public libraries, he was "a veritable Maecenas." If a library lacked a rare book, he would order a search to be made as far afield as Alexandria.

Modern historians, besides taking a favorable view of the emperor's foreign policy and his campaigns along the eastern frontier, praise Domitian's reform of the Roman judicial system and his administration of the civil service. Among those he appointed to high office were Quintilian, Pliny the Younger, and Domitian's greatest historical enemy, Tacitus — a fact for which both Pliny and Tacitus found it necessary to apologize.

Domitian, at least in his earlier years, was also a stern domestic moralist. Although his personal life was reportedly dissolute, he refused to countenance the sins of others. He decreed that the Vestal Virgin Cornelia, who had been convicted of unchastity, should be punished *more maiorum* — according to the ancestral mode — that is to say, should be entombed alive. Meanwhile, loose women were forbidden to ride on litters, and slave dealers to provide the markets with a supply of newly gelded eunuchs. During a time of food shortage, he made a determined attack on the Italian winegrowers, whose vineyards swallowed up the cornfields, ordering that no further vines should be planted in Italy and that, in the provinces, the acreage devoted to wine pro-

In this detail from the Cancelleria Reliefs (which provide a three-dimensional record of Emperor Domitian's life), the aging Vespasian places his right hand upon his younger son's shoulder in an approving gesture that signifies the solidarity and continuity of the Flavian dynasty. Domitian's hapless reign was to be punctuated by a series of scandals involving his faithless wife, Domitia, whose plump likeness appears on the first-century coin below.

duction should be rigorously cut down.

The change that overtook him was apparently gradual. As a young man, Domitian had hated blood. But "his good will and self-restraint," observes Suetonius, "were not . . . destined to continue long," and presently a sadistic strain appeared. Yet the extent of Domitian's "reign of terror" may perhaps have been exaggerated. After his death, three formidable adversaries combined to blot his reputation — Tacitus, Pliny, and the early Christian Church. Tacitus and Pliny detested Domitian because he had brutalized their own class, the privileged senatorial order, and during his reign had succeeded in decimating the entire Roman aristocracy; the Christians, because he was thought to have instigated the notorious Second Persecution.

When that persecution finally broke out, the Christian Church had been enjoying a quarter-century of peace and progress — ever since Nero's persecution ordered as reprisal for their alleged role in setting the great fire of 64. Christians, at the time, were apt to speak with approval both of Vespasian and of Titus and to regard them as *suavissimi principes* — delightful princes — who, by their destruction of Jerusalem, had "revenged Christ upon the Jews." But during the last years of Domitian's reign, the old laws aimed at professing Christians, which had seldom been enforced under Vespasian and Titus, were reapplied with some severity. According to modern historians, the Christian accounts of Domitian's persecution may well have been a little far-fetched. It was "not a general persecution at all," one authority assures us, "but a series of isolated acts directed against a few influential persons," among whom were various members of the emperor's family. Where-

ever the truth may lie, there is no evidence to support the claim that, toward the end of Domitian's life, the Colosseum ran with Christian blood.

Yet Domitian's last years were grim and horrible enough. He had once remarked — a remark quoted with admiration by the virtuous Emperor Marcus Aurelius — that rulers were bound to be unhappy men, since nobody would believe that conspirators threatened their lives until the conspiracy had found its victim. Astrologers had already told Domitian that he was to die a violent death and had even warned him when and how. That, at least, was the popular Roman story. And there seems no doubt that, as he grew older, Domitian slowly developed into a dangerous paranoiac. He had abandoned his former literary pursuits, and the only books he read were the notebooks and memoirs of the gloomy Emperor Tiberius. His daily exercise he took in a gallery lined with highly polished stone, which would reflect any assailant who attempted to creep up behind his back. Naturally, as his end approached, there was the usual crop of portents. Lightning flashes struck the Temple of the Flavians, the palace, and even the emperor's bedroom, and a hurricane tore the inscription from the base of an imperial statue.

By that time, his friends and servants, with the assent of his wife, Domitia, had actually arranged to murder him. The time had been fixed, and the assassin chosen. On the eve of the appointed day, the emperor received a present of apples, and he handed them over to his attendants, saying merely: "Let's have them tomorrow — if tomorrow ever comes." The morrow came, but that evening when Domitian returned from the bath, Stephanus, a member of his niece's household, pretending that he had unearthed a conspiracy, was admitted to Domitian's presence. As the emperor was scanning a fictitious list of conspirators, Stephanus suddenly stabbed him in the groin. Suetonius tells of his last struggle:

Domitian put up a good fight. The boy who was . . . attending to the household gods in the bedroom, witnessed the murder and later described it. . . . On receiving the first blow, Domitian grappled with Stephanus, and screamed at the boy to hand him the dagger which was kept under his pillow and then run for help; the dagger, however, proved to have no blade, and the doors to the servants' quarters were locked. Domitian fell on top of Stephanus and, after cutting his own fingers in an effort to disarm him, began clawing at his eyes; but succumbed to seven further stabs, his assailants being a subaltern named Clodianus, Parthenius' freedman Maximus, Satur a head-chamberlain, and one of the Imperial gladiators. He died at the age of forty-four, on September 18th, 96 A.D. . . .

The fallen tyrant was no unsightly monster, but a handsome, well-built personage, with a fresh skin — he was apt to blush quickly, upon the smallest provocation — and large, but somewhat weak eyes. His look was "not at all imperious," and until he grew bald his only obvious blemish was that he had awkward hammertoes. He became extremely sensitive about his baldness and disliked any reference to bald men, though for his own amusement he composed a learned manual on the preservation of the hair.

With Domitian, the Flavian dynasty, which had begun so well, came to a tragic and disgraceful end. He was succeeded by Marcus Cocceius Nerva, a high-minded legalist, chosen for his personal virtues and for his well-known constitutional sympathies by a Roman Senate that dreaded the appearance of another absolute monarch. During his brief reign, from 96 to 98, Nerva revised the fiscal system, reformed the land laws, and tolerated the Christian faith. But when the Praetorian Guard threatened to rise in revolt and summarily executed some of Domitian's murderers, Nerva decided that the conduct of the empire needed a younger and steadier hand. He then adopted as his heir and coregent an energetic Spanish general, Marcus Ulpius Trajanus, the first of the four enlightened sovereigns of the Antonine dynasty — Trajan, Hadrian, Antoninus Pius, and Marcus Aurelius — who gave Romanized Europe just over eighty years of unexampled peace and grandeur.

II

THE BLOODY SPECTACLE

The history of the Roman world is written not only in its books, statues, inscriptions, and the tremendous buildings that it raised, but in the coins, large and small, of bronze, silver, or fine gold, each bearing an emperor's portrait and title, that flowed incessantly from the imperial mint. As Alexander Pope once pointed out, a coin can provide a far more lasting record than the most ambitious piece of masonry:

Ambition sigh'd; she found it vain to trust
The faithless Column and the crumbling Bust;
Huge moles, whose shadows stretched from shore to shore,
Their ruins ruin'd, and their place no more!
Convinc'd, she now contracts her vast design,
And all her Triumphs shrinks into a Coin . . .
A small Euphrates thro' the piece is rolled,
And little Eagles wave their wings in gold.

When a coin was circulated, it carried an official message into the farthest regions of the empire. Every emperor made full use of the opportunity his coinage offered. Nero, for example, proclaimed his military virtues by producing a splendid coin that displayed the laureled head of Caesar on one side and on the other showed him attending the grand maneuvers of his guard. Another coin reminded his subjects how generously he had reconstructed Rome after the terrible fire of 64. Again the obverse bears the sovereign's image; the reverse, a detailed representation of the magnificent produce market that he had built amid the city's ruins.

Vespasian, too, struck a series of coins designed to immortalize his own achievements. Special attention was paid to the emperor's victorious campaign against the Jews; on one coin, under the legend *Judaea Capta*, is a figure that symbolizes conquered Jewry mourning head in hand beneath a palm. Vespasian also wished to commemorate his restoration of the Temple of Jupiter on the Capitoline Hill, burned down in the recent civil war; while Titus was particularly proud of his work on the vast amphitheater begun by his father. As we know, the Colosseum was completed by Titus's younger brother, Domitian — though Titus held the opening ceremonies in the still unfinished edifice during the year 80, celebrating this memorable occasion with a lavish gladiatorial show that lasted for a hundred days.

Titus's coin depicts the new amphitheater soon after its inauguration. That the design might be all the more effective, the arena has been tilted sideways like a basket to show the prodigious concourse of spectators closely packed upon three different levels. Around its façade, statues and groups of statuary fill every space between the piers, and beside the structure rises a lofty fountain known as the Meta Sudans, or the Sweating Meta. The *meta*, which the fountain appeared to resemble, was the tall post that marked the end of the race track in the Roman circus, and down the flanks of the conical centerpiece flowed a stream of glistening water.

Such is our earliest pictorial record of the Flavian Amphitheater, and perhaps it is not entirely accurate, though it conveys well enough a contemporary artist's impressions of the building's general bulk and dignity. Why, in the first place, did it become known as the Colosseum? Probably the name was a tribute to the amphitheater's gigantic size, but some historians think that it may have referred to a colossal statue of Nero, which stood nearby and must have been incorporated in the decorations of the Golden House. Remodeled by his successors, who made it into a statue of the sun-god

by adding the appropriate solar crown, this "crowned colossus" continued to stand at least until the middle of the fourth century.

When Domitian completed the Colosseum, Nero's notorious palace had not yet been torn down. But, although both Vespasian and Titus seem to have lodged there for a time, they threw open the gardens to form a public park. It was Domitian who finally moved away, to the huge new residence — one of the masterpieces of Roman architecture — that he had reared upon the Palatine. The Golden House had become an empty shell, and after part of the building complex had been destroyed by fire, the Emperor Trajan (98–117) decided to demolish what was left of it and raise his baths above the leveled debris.

Vespasian and Titus, when they sacrificed Nero's gardens and drained his artificial lake, were making a typically propagandist gesture. Their generosity did not pass unnoticed. "Rome has been restored to herself," wrote the poet Martial — who reached the capital from his birthplace in Spain about the year 64 and enjoyed the literary patronage of both the younger Flavians — ". . . that is now the delight of the people which was formerly a tyrant's."

Elsewhere, Martial speaks of the "far-seen Amphitheater" lifting its "mass august" upon the very site of Nero's lake. The line that Martial adopted was well-calculated to please his patrons. They were determined that the public should applaud not only their imperial splendor but also their paternal liberality. Standing near the end of the Sacred Way — down which every triumph and procession rumbled — in the midst of the broad valley between the Esquiline, the Palatine, and

A coin struck by Emperor Titus to commemorate the opening of the Colosseum in A.D. 80 shows the rows of statues that once lined its upper galleries, and — to the immediate right — the Meta Sudans, an enormous columnar fountain that originally stood alongside the edifice. Over the centuries, the arena's façade (right) has been stripped of its statuary and ornamental plaques, and its soft limestone facing has been deeply stained and corroded by the elements.

the Caelian hills, the Colosseum occupied a conspicuous position among the monuments of Rome's official quarter. Where Nero had built for his own amusement, the Flavians were planning and building for what they conceived to be the public good.

Everything about the structure betokened its permanence. Unlike the Greeks, whose genius was capable of working upon a comparatively restricted scale, the Romans valued sheer size. The vast dimensions of the new amphitheater — the largest building of its kind that yet had been raised — were certainly calculated to inspire respect. A huge elliptical edifice in four stories, over 150 feet high, it measured 620 by 513 feet and enclosed an oval arena 287 feet long by 180 feet wide.

Around the arena behind a lofty protective wall, stretched a spacious *podium*, or marble terrace. Here in magnificent ringside boxes presided such exalted personages as the emperor himself, the Pontifex Maximus, and his charges the Vestal Virgins. Above them rose tiers of marble seats, divided into two main zones: the first intended for distinguished private citizens; the second, for members of the middle class. A third zone was allocated to slaves and foreigners, and a fourth to women and the poor, who occupied wooden seats beneath a separate flat-roofed colonnade. On the roof of this gallery was posted a detachment of sailors, recruited from imperial warships; it was their task to manage the extensive *velarium*, a colored awning that was handed across the arena with ropes to protect the audience against sun and rain.

Modern archaeologists have not yet decided just how large a crowd the Colosseum held. One authority estimates as many as 50,000; but about 45,000 persons is the

The architectural cross section and elevation at left, faithfully reconstructed by Italian archaeologist Luigi Canina in 1851, provides graphic visual evidence that the amphitheater was an aesthetic as well as a technical triumph. As the large cross section at the lower right — from the 1725 edition of Carlo Fontana's L'Anfiteatro Flavio — reveals, the Colosseum's anonymous designers created two distinct seating areas: an exposed double-tier of seats for the bulk of the arena's 45,000 spectators, and a series of enclosed galleries for women, slaves, and foreigners. Another of Fontana's views (right) shows the elaborate system of guy ropes, masts, and eyes that supported the velarium, *or awning, which shielded spectators from both sun and rain.*

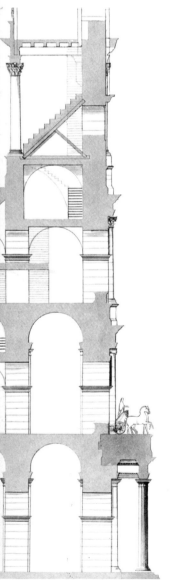

figure generally accepted by contemporary historians.

Even for a Roman architect, the construction of the amphitheater was a tremendous feat of engineering; and many different materials were combined to reinforce its massive fabric. Of these, travertine, a local limestone brought from quarries near Tivoli along a road that had been specially made for the purpose, evidently performed the most important function. The builders of the Colosseum seem to have adopted very much the same principles as are now employed by architects who work in steel and ferroconcrete. Using travertine blocks, they raised a skeleton framework of concentric piers and arches, then linked the travertine rings with a series of connecting lateral walls — on the upper floors in brick and concrete, on the lower in tufa or volcanic stone; the vaults were constructed of pumice stone, which tended to reduce their weight.

Externally, apart from its statues — no doubt a rather unfortunate addition — the Colosseum was severely plain. Each of three lower stories formed a monumental arcade, divided by columns of a single order — Doric, Ionic, or Corinthian. The fourth story was set with Corinthian pilasters, and a range of narrow quadrangular windows (which lighted the passage behind the gallery) pierced the wall between every other pair. Here again the material employed was travertine, and because the masons did not use mortar, they inserted iron clamps to hold the blocks in place.

The amphitheater had no less than eighty entrances; and of these seventy-six bore numbers that corresponded to numbers stamped on the spectators' tickets. Two were reserved for the emperor and his suite and led directly to the podium; two, for the gladiators themselves, who

like the heroes of the modern bull ring, always entered in procession. One of the latter was a small, forbidding entry named the Porta Libitinaria — after Libitina, the Roman goddess of death — through which the bodies of the slain were hurried out toward an unmarked grave.

The whole area surrounding the Colosseum had been paved and railed off. From a broad approach, cobbled with slabs of lava, one entered a precinct with a pavement of travertine more than five thousand feet wide, encompassed by substantial boundary stones, a few of which remain standing. It was then an easy journey, under the numbered portal, up a broad staircase, and thence to a numbered landing and a numbered seat.

The ingenious architects of the Colosseum had carefully studied the spectator's needs. Having entered without undue jostling and crowding, he could settle down to enjoy, in comfort, a long exciting day of sport and pageantry, which began at dawn and, during the reigns of Domitian and other gladiatorial enthusiasts, lasted far into the night. Overhead stretched the protective *velarium*; below, at the broadest extent of the ellipse, reclined the emperor and his assembled dignitaries; beyond them stretched the surface of the arena, which was often remodeled and planted with trees and rocks to resemble an exotic landscape — a background for one of the *venationes,* or wild beast hunts, that frequently accompanied the gladiatorial games. Beneath the arena was a labyrinth of lightless cells that housed prisoners and beasts condemned to die, and an elaborate system of elevators that raised them as their turns came.

When the first audience poured into the Colosseum for the inaugural festivities of the year 80 — marveling at the size and splendor of the uncompleted edifice —

the strange institution that it had been designed to serve was already nearly two hundred years old, if we date the beginning of the gladiatorial games from the earliest official performance, organized by the two consuls of the year, in 105 B.C. But the games as a religious institution had an even longer history.

The Romans were always great borrowers. During their conquest of Italy, the most formidable opponents they had encountered were the ancient Etruscan people, whose homeland lay northwest of Rome, including part of Umbria and the whole of modern Tuscany. A gifted, mysterious race, the Estruscans — as the paintings in their tombs reveal — combined a passionate devotion to the ordinary pleasures of life with a haunting fear of death. They were cruel, too, and deeply superstitious. The powers of the underworld, they felt, needed constant propitiation; and they were accustomed to sacrifice prisoners of war, particularly the Roman prisoners they captured, to the unquiet spirits of the slain. Sometimes their victims were ordered to fight among themselves until the last had fallen.

Far more sophisticated than the people who conquered them, the Etruscans, even in losing their nationhood, made a peculiarly deep impression upon Roman ways of life and thought. It was from them that Romans learned to divine the future by observing the flight of birds and studying the entrails of sacrificial beasts, and from them that they took the ivory curule chair, the ruler's gilded wreath and purple robe, and the *fasces,* or bundles of rods fastened about an axe, that the lictors carried in processions.

The Etruscans also contributed the gladiatorial games, a form of human sacrifice originally associated

This vigorous bronze statuette is clad in full gladiatorial regalia. The short sword, square shield, plumed helmet, and bare torso mark him as a contestant of the Samnite class.

with the solemn rites surrounding death. Once the games were transferred to Rome, however, they gradually lost their true religious meaning and, under the pressure of the Roman social system, were adapted to a very different purpose. That purpose was the gratification of an enormous urban proletariat, which demanded that it should be richly amused as well as sheltered, bathed, and fed.

Every Roman dynast since the last days of the republic had competed with his political rivals in providing splendid shows. In 65 B.C., Julius Caesar, for example, collected so large a troop of gladiators that his adversaries, we learn from Suetonius, rushed a bill through the Senate, obliging him to reduce the number of combatants to just over two hundred pairs. But he had his revenge in 46 B.C., after he had defeated Pompey, by presenting a miniature holocaust that involved a thousand ordinary gladiators, sixty mounted men, and forty elephants. Caesar, at least, had not completely forgotten the original significance of the games, which to the end were called both *ludi,* or games, and *munera,* or offerings. One display was offered to his father's memory, a second to that of his daughter.

The religious tradition died hard. Even in imperial days, the attendant who ran up to a fallen gladiator and established the fact of his death by a blow upon the forehead was arrayed either as Charon, the Etruscan minister of fate, carrying Charon's emblematic hammer; or as Hermes Psychopompos, the Hellenic divinity who conducted the spirits of the dead down into the underworld. And then there was the presence of the Pontifex Maximus and of the aristocratic Vestal Virgins to sanctify the bloody business. The emperor, himself a demigod, not only presided over the audience but sometimes shared in their excitement, like Claudius shouting at the gladiators or Titus arguing with the crowd.

A parade of chariots opened the spectacle. In each rode a contestant, wearing a purple, gold-embroidered cloak. Dismounting, the gladiators formed a procession that circled around the huge arena, and when he reached the emperor's box, each man threw out his right arm, uttering the proud and defiant cry: *"Ave, imperator, morituri te salutant!"* (Hail, emperor, men soon to die salute thee). Suetonius records that once, on the occasion of a mimic sea fight, the Emperor Claudius, a notoriously impulsive and unstable person, answered the gladiators' claim that they were "soon to die" by vulgarly shouting back "or maybe not" — which so offended and unnerved the future victims that they threatened to break off the show. For the gladiatorial corps, though largely recruited from condemned criminals and prisoners of war, had a strong sense of professional dignity.

Behind the gladiators as they marched around the arena came slaves who exhibited the contestants' helmets and weapons. The gladiatorial helmet was a particularly splendid piece of workmanship, with its pierced visor covering the whole face, its lofty ridge, which frequently bore a crest of ostrich plumes or peacock feathers, and its wide, elegantly angled brim.

During the imperial age, the Roman gladiator usually belonged to one of four main classes. First came the heavily armed Samnite, whose equipment had been adapted from that of the formidable Samnite warriors encountered and vanquished by Rome in the early days of the republic. The Samnite carried a sword or a lance and the *scutum*, a shield not unlike the large quadrangular shield carried by a Roman legionary. His chest was naked, but besides his tremendous helmet he wore a protective covering on his right arm and massive armor upon his left leg. Second was the less elaborately armed Thracian, with his *sica*, a curved short sword, and *parma*, or buckler, that might be either square or round. Third was the Myrmillo, or fishman, so-called because he had a fish-shaped crest. He was customarily chosen to engage the fourth class of gladiator, the *retiarius*, or net-wielder.

The man with the net was the most lightly armored of all. His face, head, chest, and legs were entirely unprotected, though a broad leather belt covered the lower part of his trunk and, bound to his left arm, was a heavy shoulder piece. His business was to dart in, evading the *secutor's* strokes, and once he had entangled the heavier and clumsier man in his net, drive home his massive three-pronged spear. If his casts at first proved unsuccessful, a cord attached to his lethal net would help him snatch it back again.

Such were the chief contestants, but the Roman gladiatorial corps included many lesser types of combatants: boxers, archers, horsemen, men who fought from chariots, and the highly trained *bestiarii*, who only appeared in the popular wild beast hunts. These tough professionals, however, were very seldom employed during the early stages of the show.

A typical day in the Flavian Amphitheater began with a succession of bloodless duels, often comic or fantastic. The contestants might be women, dwarfs, or cripples, and the weapons they used were frequently made of wood. Then a sonorous blast on the *tuba*, or war trum-

pet, heralded the opening of the main performance. Every sword and pike had been carefully tested for sharpness. The gladiators were escorted into the ring by a troop of busy managers, who, should a fighter seem too timid or too lazy and cautious, loudly urged, and sometimes lashed, him forward.

Meanwhile the crowd that packed the slopes of the amphitheater — from the distinguished spectators on the marble *podium* to the mob beneath the gallery — was growing more and more tumultuous. Strains of music often accompanied the show — there were occasions when an hydraulic organ was played — but the music must soon have been lost in the savage hubbub produced by 45,000 maddened sportsmen, each bellowing his delight or dismay as he watched the varying fortunes of a different pair of duelists. Some of the spectators' cries have come down to us: *"Habet!"* (That's done for him!), *"Hoc habet!"* (Now he's had it!). Simultaneously, the excited managers, supported by slaves who wielded leather thongs or even brandished red-hot bars, were yelling out their own instructions: *"Iugula!"* (Kill!), *"Verbera!"* (Strike!), *"Ure!"* (Burn the fellow up!). Whenever a man dropped, Saint Augustine relates, the whole mass of fiercely attentive spectators gave utterance to a general roar.

The ceremonies that attended defeat were particularly strange and poignant. The fallen gladiator appealed for mercy by throwing away his shield and raising a finger of his left hand; then, unless the emperor himself were present, it was his victorious adversary who either spared or condemned him. (Now and then, a gladiator was finished off by a man he had previously saved, and there is an epitaph to a fallen gladiator in which he advises those who come after him to beware of such displays of clemency: "Take warning from my fate. Give no quarter, whoever the fallen may be!") In the sovereign's presence, the crowd advised their ruler. Waving cloths and displaying upturned thumbs, they shouted "*Mitte!*" (Let him go free); or by turning down their thumbs, they vociferated "*Iugula!*" — recommending that the fallen man should pay the penalty. When the emperor happened to share their feelings, he confirmed the crowd's verdict and granted the defeated gladiator's plea, or with *pollice verso,* downturned thumb, ordered his immediate execution.

At the end of the show, lists were prepared of the gladiators who had taken part. The letter *P* meant that a man had perished; the letter *V* that he had vanquished his foe; while *M* (for *missus,* or sent off) indicated that he had lost his duel but had been allowed to depart unscathed through the Porta Sanivivaria. The triumphant survivor of many fights ultimately became a hero. After a victorious conflict, he received magnificent rewards and, followed by the cheers of the crowd, ran from the amphitheater, holding a palm branch or wearing a victor's crown and carrying a silver dish on which was heaped his prize money.

Naturally, a victorious gladiator was much admired by women, and popular inscriptions — the *graffiti* that cover the walls of Roman and Pompeian buildings — speak of the privileges he obtained and the romantic passions he inspired, as "*decus puellarum, suspirium puellarum*" (the delight and sighed-for joy of girls). It was said that certain aristocratic ladies had now and then sought the embraces of a gladiatorial champion;

and there were those who believed that the Emperor Commodus (180–192), who himself appeared in the games, had been begotten by a gladiator. Some women went so far as to elope with the hero they had chosen. The infatuated Eppia, described in one of Juvenal's satires, elected to run off with a battered brute who was neither young nor good-looking but had a face that showed the scars of his helmet, a crippled arm, a wart on his nose, and perpetually moist and running eyes. "But gladiators are more comely than any Adonis. Him it is she prefers to children, country, sister; him she sets above her husband. It is the sword these women cherish."

So fascinated by the sport were women like Eppia that they would sometimes learn the gladiatorial trade. During the year 63, Tacitus informs us, gladiatorial games were held "on a no less magnificent scale than before, but exceeding all precedent in the number of distinguished women and senators disgracing themselves in the arena." Such women took their profession seriously; and Juvenal depicts these grotesque amazons going through their daily exercise, panting and sweating as they learned to thrust and parry, their legs heavily swaddled in bandages, grunting under the weight of a helmet, and slashing at a dummy with their wooden swords. Both Nero and Domitian (who arranged torch-lit exhibitions of their skill) patronized the women gladiators, and these unusual combatants retained their vogue for almost a century and a half, until by decree of the Emperor Septimius Severus, women gladiators were at length prohibited in the year 200.

Perhaps it was the frivolity of the spectacle, rather than its cruelty or its indecency, that offended the taste

of the serious-minded Septimius Severus. Before Christianity became the religion of the empire in 330, the gladiatorial games had comparatively few critics; and a multitude of high-minded patriots defended the institution as a nursery for the ancient Roman virtues, in which discipline, courage, and endurance were daily taught with the help of blood and suffering. Thus authority had always upheld the sport, and how to furnish a constant supply of men and beasts was a problem that faced successive rulers. Most of the gladiators were recruited from the ranks of convicts and prisoners of war, although impoverished free men and broken-down aristocrats — like Sempronius, a descendant of the Gracchi whom Juvenal describes scudding fearfully around the arena in the costume of the *retiarius* — sometimes chose a gladiator's life.

Drafted into gladiatorial schools, the men received a long and strenuous training. These schools were scattered all over the empire, and there were no less than three at Rome itself. The gladiators' barracks at Pompeii consisted of a two-story structure built around a large courtyard; and besides the grim little rooms in which the men were lodged and fed, it included windowless cells where the recalcitrant prisoner, shackled with heavy leg irons, had scarcely room to stand up. But a gladiator's health was well cared for. He was trained on a strengthening diet of barley, and his wounds received the best attention. Galen, the most famous physician of the Roman world, who afterward entered the service of the Emperor Marcus Aurelius, had begun his career and gained much valuable experience during his early life at a gladiatorial school.

Revolts were not unknown; it was from the school at Capua that Spartacus and his companions broke out in the year 73 B.C. A native of Thrace — who had served as a Roman legionary but had deserted to become a bandit and then, after his capture, had been obliged to learn the gladiatorial trade — Spartacus was evidently a born leader. Armed with kitchen knives, he and seventy fellow prisoners battled their way out of the school, routed the soldiers pursuing them, and reached the crater of Vesuvius which at the time was still dormant.

When they were besieged in the crater, Spartacus and his party managed to escape by letting themselves down the face of the cliffs on primitive ladders made from twisted wild vines. Their numbers grew. Shepherds, herdsmen, and fugitive slaves now poured in to join the insurrection and ravage the farms and towns of southern Italy. Meanwhile, Spartacus hammered his tattered contingent into a powerful fighting force. A man of high intelligence, he did not expect that he could permanently defeat Rome; his plan was to clear a road north and escape to freedom through the Alpine passes. On nine occasions, he worsted Roman commanders. Not only did he show magnificent leadership, but he seems also to have displayed an unexpected strain of generosity, doing his best to protect the terrified country people against his plundering and raping followers.

Spartacus's revolt lasted two years, from 73 to 71 B.C. It was at length suppressed by the millionaire politician Marcus Licinius Crassus who, after several reverses, blockaded the rebels in the southern tip of Italy, where Spartacus died a warrior's death and his army was annihilated. Roman vengeance took a peculiarly hideous form. After the destruction of Spartacus, six thousand of his men perished on crucifixes, which lined the Appian

Way between Capua and Rome. Historians and novelists alike have drawn a flattering picture of the heroic ex-slave. We must not forget, however, that Spartacus himself had revived an ancient gladiatorial practice and, to appease the spirit of a fallen friend, once ordered three hundred of his Roman prisoners to engage in mortal combat.

Rome had learned a lesson that it would never forget. Spartacus, with a few desperate followers, had defied the whole republic, and it had required two years of fighting and the use of ten legions to restore Rome's shaken dignity. Thenceforward Roman governments were always wary of the gladiators and took special precautions to prevent too many gladiators from belonging to private persons. In periods of emergency, bellicose politicians were also kept away from the gladiatorial schools. During the early empire, both Caligula and Claudius appointed an official charged with the organization of the games. But there could be no question of curtailing the sacred games themselves or of controlling the lucrative traffic in human raw material, which had already assumed monstrous proportions by the beginning of the first century A.D.

Agents toured the empire, purchasing likely men and collecting rare and handsome animals. A particularly repulsive aspect of the shows in the amphitheater was the famous wild beast hunts. Trained animals were sometimes put through their paces. Much more often beasts were driven into the amphitheater from their underground dens merely to be chased and slaughtered. The *bestiarii,* professional beast slayers, fought with lions, tigers, bears, and bulls. A wonderfully graphic sketch found in the Colosseum, scratched on a convenient slab of masonry, shows two half-naked spearsmen attacking six ferocious bears; and a mosaic of the fourth century depicts a large-scale hunting scene in which an intrepid gladiator named Serpennius, who has neither leg armor nor helmet, transfixes on the point of his lance the rearing leopard that has almost brought him down.

Far worse, however, was the destruction of harmless animals — ostriches, giraffes, and deer. Roman spectators delighted in bloodshed; there can be no other explanation of their favorite public pastime. Even the good-natured Emperor Titus, at the inauguration of the Colosseum, provided, according to Suetonius, "a most lavish gladiatorial show . . . and a wild beast hunt, five thousand beasts of different sorts dying in a single day." Similarly, Trajan, during the course of two days, witnessed the slaughter of nearly three thousand animals. And late in the second century, a high official who afterward became emperor staged a hunt that involved three hundred ostriches and two hundred Alpine chamois. The quarry in these wild beast hunts was expected to die a brutal death; and there is an inscription recording a *venatio,* which speaks of ten bears as having been disposed of *crudeliter,* with the right degree of cruelty.

Before *venationes* were finally abolished — which was not until the sixth century — many noble species of wild animals had vanished from the Roman Empire: North Africa had lost its elephants; Nubia, its hippopotami; Mesopotamia, the powerful lions we admire in Assyrian bas-reliefs; Hyrcania, its famous Caspian tigers. All had been chased out of their natural habitat or slaughtered for the delectation of a Roman audience.

Ancient Rome's less bloodthirsty sports, held in other

public buildings, rivaled the popularity of those held in the Colosseum, although they served the same purpose — that of keeping the urban proletariat safely occupied and entertained. It was a gigantic task. During the age of the Antonines, well over a million inhabitants are thought to have crowded into Rome, and of these at least 150,000 were permanently unemployed. Their existence was a long unbroken vacation; by modern standards, even the working citizen would seem to have enjoyed a life of leisure. In the reign of Claudius, 150 days were celebrated as regular holidays, 93 being given up to games; in addition, there were solemn religious feasts and imperial parades and triumphs.

It is not surprising, therefore, that — although a great procession of temples, enriched with gold and polished marble, looked down upon the Sacred Way — some of the finest buildings in Rome should have been devoted to amusement. Not only did the emperor construct magnificent baths — where his subjects steamed and soaked throughout the day — and spacious porticoes and colonnades — each a miniature museum of art, where they lolled and talked at ease — but in addition to the amphitheater, he provided the theater and the circus. The Circus Maximus alone, after its rebuilding by Julius Caesar, could hold 150,000 persons, and it was again enlarged, in the early empire, to admit another 100,000. Among other circuses were the Circus Flaminius, built during the republic; the Circus Gai, raised by Caligula; and Domitian's Circus Agonalis, on the site of the present Piazza Navona.

Blood was frequently shed in the circus, as when Pompey sent a troop of barbarian gladiators to contend with twenty infuriated elephants that nearly broke

down the protective railings. But the chief object of the Circus Maximus was to accommodate the chariot races — hence its tremendous length, steadily extended by successive rulers until, during Trajan's reign, it was some 1,800 feet long and 600 feet wide.

Just as Titus had employed the currency to commemorate his inauguration of the Colosseum, so Trajan minted a handsome coin to advertise his reconstruction of the circus, one that showed both its stately exterior and the general arrangement of the race track. Like the Colosseum, it had a fine arcaded frontage, and beneath the lowest arcades were the shops that sold food and wine and also the lodgings of prostitutes and soothsayers. Inside the circus, one can see the *spina*, or backbone, around which the charioteers raced, with a *meta*, or post, at either end, and seven huge eggs and seven brazen dolphins — which were moved to indicate the progress of the race — arranged symmetrically along its ridge. In the center of the circus was a towering obelisk — now standing in Rome's Piazza del Popolo — a memorial to the glory of Ramses II, brought back from Egypt by Augustus.

In festive splendor, if not in solemn grandeur, the Circus Maximus must have outshone the Colosseum. The track itself was strewn with glistening sand; the manes of the horses were threaded with pearls. Helmeted jockeys, each wearing the colors of his "faction" — white, green, red, or blue — drove into sight from the *carceres*, or stables, surrounded by a half-dozen servants. At a signal from the presiding magistrate, who carried an ivory staff and wore a purple toga and a golden wreath, the jockeys sent their two-, three-, or four-horse chariots desperately wheeling around the course.

In his *Art of Love,* Ovid recommends the circus as a delightful place for making friends:

Nor should you neglect the horse races. Many are the opportunities that await you in the spacious Circus. No call here for the secret language of fingers; nor need you depend upon a furtive nod. Nobody will prevent you sitting next to a girl. Sit as closely as you like. That's easy enough; the seating compels it. . . . Now find an excuse to start a pleasant conversation, and begin by saying things that you can say quite audibly. Be sure you ask her whose horses are entering the ring; and, whatever her fancy may be, hasten to approve her choice. . . . If, as may well happen, a speck of dust falls into your lady's lap, brush it gently away; but, should none fall, still persist in brushing. . . . If her cloak hangs low and trails on the ground, gather it up and lift it carefully from the dirt. As a reward, she won't hesitate to allow you a glimpse of her leg. At the same time, look to the row behind and see that a stranger's knees are not pressed into her tender back. Light natures are won by little attentions. The clever arrangement of a cushion has often done a lover service. . . . Such are the advantages that the Circus offers you when you are set upon a new affair.

During the races, enormous bets were laid; and successful charioteers, like victorious gladiators, became the heroes of the public. Nero was particularly attached to their company and, as we have already seen, was accustomed to curl his hair in the fashion they affected. Many famous names have been preserved for posterity: Pontius Epaphroditus, Pompeius Musclosus, Diocles, and Scorpus, who had over two thousand wins. Usually they began their careers as slaves, but often they accumulated large fortunes, and their portraits were scribbled all over Rome on any vacant stretch of plaster. Celebrated horses, too, had their devotees, both in Rome and in the provinces. Thus, on the mosaic floor of an African bathhouse, we find a charming tribute to a favorite stallion: *"Vincas, non vincas, te amamus, Polydoxe!"* (Whether you win or whether you lose, we love you still, O Polydoxus!).

During the first and second centuries, races in the circus drew a considerably more enthusiastic crowd than performances upon the stage. But Rome possessed three enormous theaters: the theaters of Balbus, Pompey, and Marcellus, the last having been begun by Julius Caesar and completed by the Emperor Augustus in 11 B.C. Nero was passionately devoted to the stage, and Seneca, Nero's tutor and victim (his pupil eventually ordered him to commit suicide) has left us nine horrific tragedies, dramas of intrigue and crime and revenge, which had a strong, and evidently a somewhat harmful, effect upon the great Elizabethan dramatists.

Like the Elizabethans, a Roman audience always welcomed scenes of bloodshed — the banquet of Thyestes, condemned to devour his own children, or the ghastly wrath of Hercules — together with lubricious episodes of rape and incest. It also appreciated the crudest type of realism. If possible, it demanded "the real thing"; and on the Roman stage, writes a learned English historian, "the foulest tales of the old mythology, the loves of Pasiphae or the loves of Leda, were enacted to the life," with a wealth of detail that, as there were women and boys present, Ovid himself confessed that he found a little shocking.

Another popular dramatic form was the mime, a social comedy in which both actors and actresses took part and women were allowed to appear completely naked. Under Domitian the Roman drama, we are told, became particularly realistic, and a convicted criminal, replacing the tragedian, was sometimes put to death before the audience. Later, these spectacles were staged in the Colosseum, where the crowd watched Hercules mounting his funeral pyre to be actually burned alive or the bandit Laureolus expiring on a crucifix. Meanwhile the theaters were declining, and during the reign of Alexander Severus, who succeeded his cousin Heliogabalus in the year 222, the Theater of Marcellus shut its doors. Some types of theatrical performance still retained their popularity, but henceforward the amphitheater and the circus supplied most of the excitement that the Roman proletariat craved.

III

PAGAN AND CHRISTIAN

It was in October 1764 that Edward Gibbon first walked "with a lofty step" among the ruins of the Roman Forum, and not until several days later could he properly collect his thoughts. Then he reported his feelings to his father at home. He was "almost in a dream," he wrote; the city had far surpassed his expectations. During the whole course of history, Gibbon believed, there had never, never arisen such another people as the Romans; and "for the happiness of mankind," he hoped there never would again.

This hope the modern historian often feels he must echo. From the emergence of the republic to the gradual decline of the empire, Roman history is both profoundly moving and peculiarly disturbing. It is a subject that reveals the human spirit at its bravest and its strongest, yet simultaneously — there is a close connection between Roman virtues and vices — at its darkest and its least attractive. Every famous building has some symbolic significance, and the Colosseum, which symbolizes Roman greatness, also typifies the strain of savage cruelty that seems to have been deeply rooted in the national character.

This strain had already become apparent during the heyday of the young republic. Under the empire, moralists looked back to the republic as a period of noble thinking and austere living. Yet Cato the Elder (234–149 B.C.), who personified the virtues of his age, recommended that the Roman landowner get rid of old tools, old cattle, and old or sickly slaves, "and whatever else is superfluous," the moment they are worn out. The stern domestic duties that Cato continued to preach were founded in the last resort on strength and avarice.

Nor, when the republican system had begun to break

down at the end of the second century B.C., do we find much evidence of human kindness. We scarcely expect it from the dictators Marius and Sulla — Marius, an unlettered proletarian who "never sacrificed to the Graces," and Sulla, the ferocious aristocrat whose complexion, mottled by high living, is said to have resembled that of a ripe mulberry sprinkled with a pinch of flour. Julius Caesar, on the other hand, was an amusing, elegant, and extremely cultivated man. Yet, in Gaul, he ruthlessly practiced genocide; and unlike his rival Pompey, he almost invariably killed his captives after a triumph. A story told by Suetonius illustrates Caesar's interpretation of the word "mercy." As a comparatively young man, he was taken at sea by pirates who "kept him prisoner for nearly forty days, to his intense annoyance." An unwilling occupant of their seaside stronghold, he soon became their friend and tutor, joined in their sports, read them his poems and speeches (abused their bad taste if his audience were inattentive), and when they were noisy and he had decided to go to sleep, immediately sent them a message through his servant, commanding them to hold their tongues. But he often "smilingly swore" that once his ransom had been paid and he had regained his freedom, he would have them all crucified. Being Caesar, he kept his word. Suetonius adds, however, that "even in avenging wrongs he was by nature most merciful"; and before the pirates were hoisted onto their crosses, he ordered that their throats should be cut.

Thus the seeds of cruelty that may have been sown by the Etruscans grew and flourished in the climate of Roman life. The taste for blood, whether conscious or unconscious, became an inseparable part of the tough, coarse-fibred Roman nature, and it was already well-developed in the lifetimes of the major Latin poets: Lucretius, who insisted, toward the end of the last century before Christ, that "man is lord of himself" and need not fear the gods or death; Vergil, who lived from 70 to 19 B.C., one of the greatest masters of verbal harmony that the world has ever known; and the exquisite elegiac writers Catullus and Propertius, who, although they died about 54 B.C. and 15 B.C., respectively, bared their hearts with a freshness and strength of feeling that recall the most splendid achievements of nineteenth-century Romantic verse.

Yet even educated Romans were prepared to accept the gladiatorial games, if not for the excitement they provided, at least for their traditional value. In the last century of the republic, Cicero (106–43 B.C.) alone dared to protest against some variations of this hideous pastime. "What pleasure," he demands, "can it give a civilized man to see a feeble human creature torn by a powerful wild beast or a fine animal transfixed by a hunting spear?" He is referring to the bloody *venationes,* but he seems not to have objected quite so strenuously to the duels between man and man. Certainly Cicero congratulates his friend Atticus on his successful ownership of a gladiatorial troop. "I hear your gladiators are fighting magnificently," he remarks. "If you had cared to hire them out, you would have cleared your expenses on the two shows you gave."

Elsewhere Cicero praises the games because they instill contempt for pain and death. Watching the gladiators fight, we learn to regulate our own lives:

Look at gladiators, who are either ruined men or barbarians. . . . See how men, who have been well trained,

prefer to receive a blow rather than basely avoid it! How frequently it is made evident that there is nothing they put higher than giving satisfaction to their owner or to the people! . . . What gladiator of ordinary merit has ever uttered a groan or changed countenance? . . . Such is the force of training, practice and habit. Shall then the Samnite, filthy fellow . . . be capable of this, and shall a man born to fame have any portion of his soul so weak that he cannot strengthen it by systematic preparation?

In the second century A.D., Pliny the Younger agreed with Cicero that the games might teach a salutary moral lesson. But Seneca, who had done his best to improve Nero's mind, without much effect upon his pupil's character, expressed a far more sympathetic point of view. Humanity, he believed, was sacred, yet men were being killed in sport! Seneca had been particularly disgusted by the contests held at the amphitheater during the slack hour of noon, when most of the audience had retired to eat and the place was half empty. Such a show he happened to have attended, expecting, he says, "some fun, wit, and relaxation — an exhibition at which men's eyes have respite from the slaughter of their fellow men. But it was quite the reverse."

In fact, what Seneca saw that noon hour was "pure murder. The men have no defensive armor. They are exposed to blows at all points, and no one ever strikes in vain." The men he watched being slaughtered were evidently condemned criminals, but that, he felt, in no way excused the spectacle. Granted the victim was a robber or a murderer, "what crime have *you* committed — that you should deserve to sit and see this show." The amphitheater had a generally corrupting influence. No amusement, he concluded, was "so damaging to good

character as the habit of lounging at the games, for then it is there that vice steals subtly upon one through the avenue of pleasure.... I come home more greedy, more ambitious, more voluptuous, and even more cruel and inhuman — because I have been among human beings."

Oddly enough, it is a zealous Christian writer who, late in the fourth century, gives us the most convincing account of the insidious fascination that the games exerted. Saint Augustine had enjoyed the pleasures of the pagan world before his conversion to the Christian faith, and he remained a remarkably acute analyst of the lawless feelings he had put behind him. Just as he probes deep into the nature of illicit love and sexual jealousy, so he describes how his friend and countryman Alypius had succumbed to the wild excitement of a gladiatorial show on his first visit to Rome. Alypius was already a Christian convert. He had come to Rome to study law, and some of his fellow law students, while they were on their way home from a dinner party, had "dragged him with friendly force" into the amphitheater despite his "strong objections and resistance."

Once there, Alypius decided to shut his eyes. "Would that he had been able to stop up his ears, too!" For when a gladiator fell and an immense roar from the whole audience rolled around the amphitheater, he was overcome by curiosity. Convinced that he had sufficient strength of mind to resist temptation, he then opened his eyes, "and was wounded more seriously in his soul than the gladiator, whom he lusted to observe, had been wounded in the body." Gazing at the bloodshed beneath him, the young Christian was infected by the spectators' furious passions. He could no longer avert his gaze and began to experience a fierce enjoyment.

"He himself watched; he shouted; he rose to fever heat." And when he left the amphitheater (no doubt the Colosseum), Alypius "took away with him a mad passion which prodded him not only to return with those by whom he had first been forced in, but even ahead of them and dragging in others." Christ, nevertheless, "with a most powerful hand," eventually drew him out again. "But that was long afterwards"; and meanwhile the unhappy Alypius had plunged into the depths of vice and squalor.

Alypius's behavior at the gladiatorial games was, of course, particularly shocking since the amphitheater had witnessed the execution of so many of his fellow converts. In Christian legend, the Colosseum is associated with a lengthy series of heroic deaths.

The first Christian to suffer martyrdom in the famous arena is said to have been Saint Ignatius, who is reputed to have been thrown to the lions after exclaiming: "I am as the grain of the field, and must be ground by the teeth of the lions, that I may become fit for His table." Soon afterward, we are told, 115 Christians were shot down with flights of arrows.

Reports of later persecutions inform us that at the beginning of the third century a patrician named Placidus, his wife, Theophista, and their two sons were roasted in a brazen bull, and that in the year 253 Sempronius, Olympius, Theodolus, and Exuperia were burned alive before the statue of the sun-god, "the crowned colossus" that stood just outside the amphitheater. Other Christian luminaries thought to have been martyred in the Colosseum include Saint Prisca, Saint Martina, Saint Potitus, Saint Eleutheria, Saint Maximus, Saint Vitus, Saint Crescentina, and Saint

Modesta. But the devout chroniclers who recorded the lives of the saints did not always distinguish between fact and fiction, and some of their more fantastic anecdotes may well have been based on pious hearsay. (Indeed, in 1969 the Roman Catholic Church dropped a number of these martyrs from its liturgical calendar because there was no definite proof of their existence.)

It is clear, however, that a multitude of Christians died, and that many of them perished in the Colosseum — often, no doubt, during the second-rate show that coincided with the Romans' midday meal. Their offense was almost always the same: they had refused to confirm their loyalty to the emperor by making a formal act of sacrifice and, no less stubbornly and grimly, had refused to deny their own religion. The best, as well as the worst, emperors believed the Christians to be a sect of dangerous revolutionaries. So, indeed, did the historian Tacitus. After describing the great fire of Rome in A.D. 64, Tacitus explains that Nero — in order to check rumors that he himself had started the conflagration — had provided scapegoats and had punished with every refinement of torture "the notoriously depraved Christians. . . ." Christ, the "originator" of the sect, Tacitus adds, "had been executed in Tiberius's reign by the governor of Judaea, Pontius Pilate. But in spite of this temporary setback the deadly superstition had broken out afresh, not only in Judaea but even in Rome. All degraded and shameful practices flourish in the capital."

Thenceforward, a series of emperors did their best to crush the hated sect. They had the weight of public opinion behind them. Both in Rome and in the provinces the most extravagant tales had long been circulated about the strange beliefs and repulsive habits of the members of this underground fraternity. The Christians, like the Jews with whom they were sometimes confused, were reported to worship an ass-headed god and were also said to practice incest, cannibalism, and other equally atrocious crimes. The Christians were inflamed, said their pagan adversaries, by an *odium generis humani,* a downright loathing of the human race, and as public enemies they at once received the blame for any calamity that might befall the empire.

Some emperors, it is true, were inclined to be lenient. Early in the second century, Pliny the Younger, then the governor of Bithynia in northwest Asia Minor, assured the Emperor Trajan that he had investigated the local Christian community and the worst he could discover about them was that they appeared to harbor a "perverse and excessive superstition," which, though certainly deplorable, did not seem quite to deserve the death sentence. And Trajan replied in moderate terms, advising against the use of police spies and hinting that, unless they gave serious trouble, the Christians should be left well alone. He agreed, however, that the governor should chasten them if they appeared to threaten public order.

That was also the view of later Roman sovereigns. Christians merited rigorous punishment not because they had embraced an outlandish and degrading superstition, but because their attitude toward authority might weaken the whole social structure. Thus Diocletian, when he set out to refashion Roman society on stern authoritarian lines, could not tolerate the existence of a sect that disregarded the divine supremacy of the emperor and obeyed a law outside Roman law. During the reign of Marcus Aurelius (A.D. 161–180), the recalcitrant Christians excited a fresh storm of hatred by refusing to take part in solemn religious rites designed to check the progress of plague, and even that humane and enlightened ruler authorized particularly savage persecutions. He, too, believed that Christianity threatened the entire imperial edifice, which, as both head of the state and priest of the state religion, he had been called upon to safeguard.

Yet Marcus Aurelius, who must have been responsible for sending thousands of Christians to a hideous death, was the only emperor who, we are told, positively disliked the gladiatorial games. He attended the amphitheater, it is said, merely from a sense of duty. Once he had taken his place on the marble *podium,* he paid as little attention as he could to the savage spectacle beneath his eyes and would quietly employ his time dictating letters to an amanuensis. For this Stoic sage, justice, courage, and temperance were the essential human virtues, and in his own life he sought not happiness but a state of inward equanimity. Marcus Aurelius — last of the "four good emperors" — was the most humane, or the least inhumane, of Roman sovereigns, and he personified all that was noblest in the ancient Roman character. It was his misfortune to be followed by a son who typified many of the national vices.

The Emperor Commodus (the first emperor since Domitian who was the natural rather than an adopted heir of his predecessor) succeeded his father in 180 and died a violent death in 192. From the beginning Commodus showed coarse and violent tastes, which gave additional coloring to the legend that he was the bastard of a gladiator, yet there is an odd resemblance between the young man's features and portrait heads of the benevolent Marcus Aurelius. They have the same slightly bulging eyes, the same distinguished length of nose and chin. But whereas Marcus Aurelius's face radiates an air of dignity and gentle sadness, with perhaps a touch of primness, from Commodus's mask glare out his vanity and cruelty and the strain of half-demented arrogance that eventually brought about his downfall.

Few more extraordinary or more unpleasant personages have ever appeared in the Colosseum. Commodus had an insensate passion for the gladiatorial games. During his father's lifetime, he adopted the profession of gladiator and had distinguished himself in the amphitheater in more than 360 duels. Before he died, he had been a contestant a thousand times, and he could claim to have become a veteran fighter. Sometimes, when he fought at home, writes his contemporary and courtier the Greek historian Dion Cassius, Commodus would actually kill his man or, while trying to clip off a strand of his hair, slice off an opponent's ear or nose:

. . . But in public he refrained from using steel and shedding human blood. Before entering the amphitheatre he would put on a long-sleeved tunic of silk, white interwoven with gold, and thus arrayed he would receive our greetings; but when he was about to go inside, he would put on a robe of pure purple with gold spangles . . . and a crown made of gems from India and of gold. . . . As for the lion-skin and club, in the street they were carried before him, and in the amphitheatre they were placed on a gilded chair, whether he was present or not. He himself would enter the arena in the garb of Mercury, and casting aside all his other garments, would begin his exhibition wearing only a tunic and unshod.

Commodus had identified himself with the demigod

A leaf from the famed Menologium of Basil II, *the elegantly illuminated service book of the Eastern Church, shows the final agonies of Saint Ignatius. The second-century Bishop of Antioch was the first Christian to be martyred on the sands of the Flavian Amphitheater.*

Hercules — hence his assumption of the ancient hero's
club and lion skin. And it is as Hercules that the emperor is represented in a famous half-length statue. To
fulfill the role of Hercules he slaughtered animals, and
with that object the amphitheater was divided up,
Dion Cassius continues, "by means of two intersecting
cross-walls which supported the gallery that ran its entire length, the purpose being that the beasts . . . might
be more easily speared at short range from any point.
In the midst of the struggle he became weary, and taking from a woman some chilled sweet wine in a cup
shaped like a club, he drank it at one gulp. At this both
the populace and we [the members of the Senate] all
immediately shouted out — 'Long life to you'."

Aiming down from the railings of the *podium,* the
emperor also shot a hundred bears. That great achieve-
ment signaled the start of the fourteen-day *ludi,* held
toward the end of Commodus's reign. Among the other
victims he accounted for were an elephant, a tiger, and
a hippopotamus. After killing them, he retired, "but,
later, after luncheon, would fight as a gladiator." Some
citizens kept away from the amphitheater; others
glanced inside and made a hurried exit. But the senators always attended and showed their admiration of
his heroic deeds. Both they and the crowd that occupied
the lower seats often felt a secret thrill of fear. No one
knew where his shafts might fall next, for a story had
gone around that, in imitation of Hercules and his slay-
ing of the Stymphalian birds, Commodus had determined to pick off a few spectators.

And here is another thing [relates Dion Cassius] that he
did to us senators. . . . Having killed an ostrich and cut
off its head, he came up to where we were sitting, holding

the head in his left hand and in his right hand raising aloft his bloody sword; and though he spoke not a word, yet he wagged his head with a grin, indicating that he would treat us in the same way. And many would indeed have perished by the sword on the spot, for laughing at him . . . if I had not chewed some laurel leaves, which I had got from my garland, myself, and persuaded the others who were sitting near me to do the same, so that in the steady movement of our jaws we might conceal the fact that we were laughing.

It was clear that Commodus was on the verge of insanity. And as usually happened when an emperor's extravagances were becoming really dangerous, a group of his friends and attendants set about destroying him. The conspirators who planned the coup were his chamberlain, the commander of his bodyguard, and his mistress Marcia. First Marcia attempted to poison him but the attempt proved unsuccessful. Then an athlete named Narcissus was sent to strangle the emperor when next he visited his private baths — and he succeeded. Commodus was only thirty-one at his death and his reign of just over twelve years brought to an end the Antonine dynasty.

The successor of Commodus was Pertinax — "an excellent and upright man," writes Dion Cassius, "but he ruled only a very short time, and was then put out of the way by the soldiers." These soldiers, the unruly Praetorian Guard, the household troops of ancient Rome, were destined to play an important part in the annals of the third century. Some historians have called this "the Praetorian period" since it was the Praetorians who determined the emperor's fate and often sold his office to the highest bidder.

Meanwhile the empire and Rome itself were changing. When, at the end of the first century A.D., Vespasian founded the Colosseum and his sons completed his work, the Sacred City was still the center of government and the chosen seat of the "divine" emperor. But once the barbarians had begun to move westward, and wave after wave of hungry tribesmen swept across the Roman frontiers, it became more and more important that the emperor personally command his armies and spend his days not on the Palatine Hill but with his men in some gloomy German outpost, if necessary. Marcus Aurelius, for example, had been obliged to pass three weary years far from the places he loved, battling along the Rhine and Danube rivers.

Many of Commodus's successors were short-lived: Pertinax (193) lasted only three months; and in one year, 238, a half-dozen Caesars were enthroned and murdered. Some of these later emperors were deplorable eccentrics, like the fourteen-year-old Syrian, Heliogabalus (218–222). The third century was indeed an age of anxiety. A series of military rulers, often foreign-born, bravely confronted their tremendous task; and the magnificent portrait heads that they left behind them, the last masterpieces of Roman sculpture, suggest the kind of men they were. They have an expression of intense, continuous strain; their brows are contracted, their foreheads deeply furrowed.

It was one of these haggard, hard-pressed emperors, Philip the Arab, son of a desert chief, who — no doubt hoping to distract attention from the empire's latest crisis — decided to celebrate the one thousandth anniversary of the foundation of the city in 248, or toward the end of 247. (The traditional date of the founding

The embattled spear-wielder shown in this detail from the renowned Borghese mosaics could well be the deranged Emperor Commodus, whose passion for unequal combat drew him to the arena more than a thousand times before his assassination in A.D. 192.

of Rome by Romulus was 753 B.C.) The background Philip chose for his millennial games was, naturally, the Colosseum. Among the beasts exhibited, and no doubt hunted to death, were lions, elephants, hippopotami, stags, antelope, and mountain goats. After five years of unremitting effort to protect the empire's increasingly unstable borders, Philip was killed in 249, battling against a rebel commander.

At last, in 284, an administrator of genius assumed the purple. Diocletian was a hardened professional soldier, the offspring of a family of Illyrian peasants, and he drastically reorganized the Roman state. Having placed himself firmly at the head of the empire, he adopted the trappings of an Eastern monarch. Petitioners were expected to kneel before him and kiss the hem of his embroidered robe; the officers of his bedchamber were servile eunuchs. Simultaneously, feeling that the burden of government was too great for any single man, he appointed three junior emperors, to each of whom he gave a separate capital. He himself presided at Nicomedia in Asia Minor. The other members of the tetrarchy ruled from Milan, from Trier on the Moselle River (modern Germany), and from Sirmium (near present-day Mitrovica, Yugoslavia).

Thus Rome itself became a venerable showplace rather than the seat of power, and for the first time Vespasian's Colosseum looked out over a gradually declining city. Diocletian's new system of taxation was beginning to destroy the existence of the independent city dwellers. Under the new bureaucracy that the emperor set up to collect these taxes and administer their disbursement, men were reduced to submissive units in the huge imperial pattern. Whether they inhabited town or country, these "slaves of the state" were forbidden to improve their condition by changing their hereditary way of life. Only the very rich were sufficiently strong to resist the government's demands. And Roman plutocrats found a means of escaping taxation by retreating from the impoverished towns to their enormous country properties, where they lived amid an army of slaves in semifeudal isolation. During the final breakdown of Roman rule, when many ancient and populous cities were completely wiped out, life on some of the vast provincial estates seems to have continued almost undisturbed.

Diocletian, who abdicated in 305 and withdrew to his fortified Dalmatian palace — where his chief occupation, he said, was planting splendid rows of cabbages — died a natural death in 313. A year earlier Constantine I, son of the tetrarch Constantius, had won the battle of the Milvian Bridge and, beneath the *Chi-Rho* sign of the Christian faith — for which he felt a warm, though as yet unfocused regard — had made himself master of the Sacred City.

It is possible that Constantine's triumphal entry of 312 was his first visit to Rome, and the imperial residence on the Palatine was duly opened to receive him. No doubt he inspected the Colosseum and the other monuments of Rome's official quarter. But now that he had recognized the conquering strength of the cross, he failed to pay his respects at the Temple of Jupiter on the Capitoline Hill. Like earlier emperors, Constantine was awarded a triumphal arch, which arose — three years after the battle of the Milvian Bridge — at the end of the Sacred Way nearest to the Colosseum. The creative impetus of Roman art was dead, or dying, in the

fourth century, and Constantine's huge and pretentious arch was embellished with pieces of sculpture torn from a variety of older monuments and inset among the mechanical productions of his own age.

Similarly, when Constantine remodeled the imposing new basilica, built by his defeated rival, Maxentius, the gigantic statue of himself, seven times larger than life, which occupied the western apse, incorporated several fragments, including an arm and a hand, that were the rightful property of previous statues. But the vast head, some six feet tall, which now stands in the Palazzo dei Conservatori, is evidently a portrait of the Christian emperor, if not of the man he was, at least of the personage he meant to be—remote, superhuman, semi-divine, with his tremendous hooked nose, boldly aggressive chin, and all-seeing, deeply cut pupils.

Upon receiving an official report—in the year 320, when he was ruling from Serdica (present-day Sofia, Bulgaria)—that the Colosseum had been struck by lightning, Constantine immediately issued orders that henceforward, when such a portentous event occurred, "written records thereof shall be very carefully collected and referred to Our Wisdom."

It is difficult to reconcile Constantine's face, or what we know of his private life and of his attitude toward his functions, with any idea of the emperor as a naturally Christian spirit. A keen supporter of the gladiatorial games during his youth and a commander who threw his German prisoners to wild beasts, Constantine executed both his wife, Fausta, and his eldest son, Crispus, by ordering that they should be slowly suffocated in the hot rooms of their bathhouses. For some while he divided his allegiance between the sun-god and the

Christian Savior, and he would appear to have valued Christian relics primarily as magic-working charms. When his British mother, the Empress Helena, let it be known that she had unearthed the "true cross" on a pilgrimage to Jerusalem, Constantine, according to one story circulated about him, appropriated the "holy nails" and had them fashioned into a handsome bit for the bridle of his favorite charger.

After his first visit to Rome, Constantine returned to the Sacred City on only three occasions. Although he beautified the fabric of the city, he had definitely abandoned it, and in 330 he founded Constantinople as the modern center of his empire. Just over a quarter of a century later, Constantine's son, Constantius II, revisiting the former capital, was obliged to adopt the role of distinguished foreign tourist.

Constantius was dazzled by Rome. But like Constantine, whenever he faced his subjects, he assumed an air of hieratic majesty, and he was careful to banish from his expression and attitude any trace of human feeling. The senators had come out to meet their sovereign; and as he approached the city, writes the fourth-century pagan historian Ammianus Marcellinus, "his calm gaze dwelt upon the courtesies offered by the senate, and so many august countenances, the very images of aristocratic ancestry." Then, turning his eyes on the crowd, "he was amazed at the numbers in which every type of mankind had flocked from all over the world to Rome."

On entering the city, "the very hearth and home of empire," Constantius was "overcome by the sheer density of miraculous creations." First, he spoke to the gathering in the senate house; next, he mounted the tribunal and addressed the crowd. Finally, he was es-

The remarkable career of Rome's first Christian monarch, Constantine I, is the subject of this ninth-century illumination. The topmost of its three registers shows the future emperor asleep; in a dream, he is inspired to affix the sign of the cross to his followers' shields before going into battle. At center, the victorious leader routs his rival Maxentius at the Milvian Bridge on the outskirts of the Eternal City; at bottom right, Saint Helena, the emperor's mother, exhibits the True Cross, which she purportedly discovered on a pilgrimage to the Holy Land.

corted up the Palatine Hill to the imperial residences that crowned its summit. At a later stage, Constantius made an extended tour of the city and its suburbs; and among the buildings he particularly admired was, of course, the Colosseum — "the huge bulk of the amphitheater, reinforced with its framework of travertine, so high that one can hardly see its top."

Other monuments the emperor found impressive were the shrines that looked down from the Capitol, "which seemed to excel in the same way as the divine excels the human"; the public baths, "almost the size of provinces"; the Pantheon, large as a "shapely city-district, vaulted over in soaring beauty"; Domitian's circus and concert hall; the Forum of Peace; and the Theater of Pompey. It was when he came to the Forum of Trajan, "which is unique in the whole world, and something even the gods . . . would regard as a marvel," that Constantius nearly dropped his mask. Pausing dumbfounded, he gazed at "the gigantic complex all around him," and said that he "would, and could, only copy Trajan's horse, which stands in the middle of the court, bearing the ruler himself." But Constantius did not leave Rome until he had ordered the erection of his own monument — the immense Egyptian obelisk, originally placed in the Circus Maximus, that today rears its sixty-foot shaft opposite St. John Lateran.

During his stay, the Eastern emperor often gratified the Roman crowd by providing chariot races, and even affected to enjoy the rowdy "back-chat of the plebs," which, although they exercised their traditional freedom of speech, luckily never went too far. In a more serious mood, he visited the pagan sanctuaries and, despite his Christian training, presided over the allocation of priesthoods and subsidized the performance of the old rites. But if Rome had astonished Constantius, he himself, with his air of divine remoteness, frequently surprised the Romans. He was a very short man, "yet he bowed down when entering high gates, and looking straight before, as though he had his neck in a vice, he turned his eyes neither to the right nor to the left, as if he had been a statue. . . ."

No less remarkable was the emperor's train of attendants. The high officers who preceded him marched beneath elaborate standards shaped like dragons — "the mouths of the dragons being open so as to catch the wind, which made them hiss as though they were inflamed with anger; while the coils of their tails were also contrived to be agitated by the breeze." Following the officers came a double row of infantry and, amid them, cavalry wearing heavy cuirasses and coats of pliant Persian mail. Every metallic surface brilliantly reflected the light, "so that you would fancy them statues polished by the hands of Praxiteles, rather than men." The Romans applauded this march past, but the spectacle was disconcerting. Rome, in the middle of the fourth century, had become a city of ghosts and illusions. It was on an Eastern potentate and his barbarian soldiers that the aging empire now depended.

IV

TWILIGHT OF THE ETERNAL CITY

Constantine the Great, having at last exchanged the imperial purple for the white robes of a Christian penitent, died in a Middle Eastern village on May 22, 337. By that time the Edict of Milan, which had granted freedom of worship to the Christians, was almost a quarter-century old; but the fierce strife between Christians and pagans lasted many years longer. It did not end until 392, when the coemperors Theodosius I and Valentinian II prohibited any form of pagan sacrifice, even the worship of the ancient household gods to whom conservative Roman families still made daily offerings of flowers and incense. Unlike earlier and more half-hearted measures, this decree had an immediate effect upon the Roman way of life. The Roman gods were finally banished, and their splendid shrines closed. "They who were once the gods of the nations," wrote Saint Jerome from his monastery at Bethlehem, "dwell with the owls and bats under their lonely roofs."

Paganism, however, had put up a valiant struggle, and pagan critics had continued to attack the new religion for its mischievous and antisocial tendencies. They noted the bitter feuds in which pious Christians engaged. No savage beasts, remarked Ammianus Marcellinus, could outdo the cruelty of Christians to one another. Worse, they seemed bent on destroying the rites and observances that, since the city's legendary foundation by Romulus, had so often saved Rome. Some of the most resolute conservatives were high officials of the empire, and among these courageous pagan diehards none is more interesting, or more closely connected with the fortunes of the Colosseum, than Quintus Aurelius Symmachus, born seven years after the Emperor Constantine's death, who was long a pillar of

Roman society and the respected leader of the Senate.

Although the fourth century was a period of immensely rich men, Symmachus's inherited fortune was comparatively modest by the standards of the day. Nevertheless, he occupied three princely houses in or near Rome and possessed thirteen huge estates, either in Italy or in the provinces, to which he occasionally paid visits. He was proud both of his noble descent and of the high position that he occupied. As leader of the Senate, he was privileged to read aloud the messages that the emperor sometimes condescended to dispatch from his distant seat of government. The emperor himself rarely came to the capital city, but Symmachus still regarded Rome as the center of the Roman universe.

The senator was also a well-known littérateur and deeply devoted to the Latin classics — though his own prose was typical of the Silver Age, clumsy, diffuse, and overornamented. He loved quoting and discussing Vergil and analyzing minor points of style. But his chief literary amusement was the composition of elaborate letters, and despite the fact that his correspondence is usually very dull indeed, it throws a vivid light on the author's state of mind and on the curiously limited outlook of his private circle.

These gentlemen of leisure could not quite believe that the Roman world was now in serious danger. Although cities were lost and provinces were ravaged, Symmachus and his literary friends remained calm. He dismissed a barbarian revolt, which had cut off Rome from the emperor's headquarters at Milan, as an isolated outbreak of brigandage that had temporarily made the roads unsafe. With terrible dramas being enacted all around him, Symmachus complains in a letter to some favored correspondent that he has very little really interesting news.

Equally limited in their opinions and tastes were other members of the fourth-century pagan aristocracy — for example, Praetextatus, a student of Aristotle and the high priest of various pagan cults, and Flavianus, whose son married Symmachus's beloved daughter. Each was a highly educated man, and with Symmachus as their brave and eloquent advocate, they conducted a long campaign to replace the winged statue of the Goddess of Victory, whose removal from its traditional altar in the Roman senate house the Emperor Constantius had ordered.

They failed, notwithstanding a learned speech delivered by Symmachus to the Emperor Valentinian II. He had always been celebrated for his "golden" oratory, and in his speech he protested that there were many ways to truth. "The Great Mystery," he cried, "cannot be approached by one avenue alone. . . . Leave us the symbol on which our oaths of allegiance have been sworn for so many generations. Leave us the system that has so long given prosperity to the State." Just as every man received a separate soul at birth, so every nation was granted a genius that presides over its destiny. Symmachus's arguments made a profound impression. He might have prevailed had not Saint Ambrose, the fiery bishop of Milan (Symmachus's cousin), immediately taken up the challenge and, by threatening Valentinian with excommunication, persuaded the emperor to reject the Senate's pleas.

Yet at the time even his opponents praised the senator's eloquence and his display of public spirit. He had numerous Christian friends, with whom he never quar-

Discovered in 1940 at Ostia near Symmachus's villa, this stately gentleman with a bundle of book rolls at his feet is commonly believed to represent the pagan statesman-scholar.

reled; and in other circumstances Symmachus himself might perhaps have made a good Christian. His moral standards were certainly high enough. He and his cultivated friends — though they led rich and stately lives — avoided any kind of sexual license. No dancing girls performed at their banquets, and they spoke with contempt of the vulgar luxuries — the dishes of lampreys and of peacocks' eggs that had once appeared on the table of a Lucullus or a Julius Caesar. Symmachus, moreover, always cherished his family — in his correspondence, he addresses his promising son as *amiabilitas tua,* your amiability, and his faithful daughter as *domina filia,* lady daughter.

Symmachus's habits were soberly old-fashioned. Yet some of the views he professed would undoubtedly have offended Cato, for he and his circle seem to have been prepared to admit that slaves themselves were human beings. "You should treat your slave as a man, even a friend," suggested the learned Praetextatus. "It is far better that he should love you than that he should fear you. . . . How often have these despised wretches shown the noblest devotion to their masters?"

Nevertheless, Symmachus warmly supported the gladiatorial games. This sensitive and delicately nurtured character found nothing at all repellent in the wholesale sacrifice of men and animals. When his youthful son was appointed to the praetorship — by then an almost meaningless office but one that every young Roman of senatorial rank was still obliged to undertake — Symmachus set about providing the necessary *munera,* or offerings, with his usual conscientious energy. They cost him the equivalent of some $190,000, and while he was organizing the show he could think of very little else.

Overleaf:
The Roman provinces had the prodigious task of providing a steady supply of exotic animals for the lavish games staged in the Colosseum and other imperial arenas. As illustrated in this colorful third-century mosaic from North Africa, the hunt was itself an extraordinary spectacle. The scene is alive with furious activity: a strong net has been erected and camouflaged inside with bushes; sheep and other domesticated animals have been penned in three projecting bays to serve as bait; and armed horsemen, assisted by beaters on foot, drive the beasts into the corral — where they are met by hunters brandishing spears and torches.

Only the bravest men and the finest animals could satisfy this anxious parent; and letters flew out to distant provinces of the empire, soliciting his friends' help. He must have charioteers and actors from Sicily, horses from Spanish studs, hounds from the wintry wastes of Scotland, lions and crocodiles from Africa. And to crown the show, from the shores of the Baltic he procured a troop of hardy German prisoners, whose determination to kill or be killed would surely satisfy a Roman audience.

Most of Symmachus's plans miscarried; his tireless enthusiasm had clearly overreached itself. Few of his Spanish horses survived the sea voyage. When the crocodiles finally reached Rome, they stubbornly refused to eat, and he was forced to have them put away. Worst of all, the Saxon gladiators conspired to disappoint his hopes; rather than die to amuse an alien crowd, they strangled one another in the darkness of their cells. Symmachus was intensely aggrieved and annoyed. He felt only a cold disgust for their uncooperative obstinacy and pig-headed barbarian courage.

Symmachus was a conservative; but since Christians could finally afford to come into the open, opponents of the games were steadily gaining ground. During the second and early third centuries, the sole critics of the ancient Roman pastime had been either writers and philosophers brought up on the art and literature of Greece, where the gladiatorial games had never really taken root, or Christian apologists like Tertullian, who contended that — whether as a sport or as a method of punishment — the spectacles were a hideous offense against humanity:

He who shudders at the body of a man who died by nature's law . . . will, in the amphitheatre, gaze down with most tolerant eyes on the bodies of men mangled, torn in pieces, defiled with their own blood; yes, and he who comes to the spectacle to signify his approval of murder being punished, will have a reluctant gladiator hounded on with lash and rod to do murder . . .

Symmachus's ill-fated games must have been among the last staged in the Colosseum. No doubt as a result of his many reverses, they were not finally held until 401. Three years later the Christian poet Prudentius solemnly adjured the Emperor Honorius to forbid a new series. Evidently the emperor refused or temporized. But soon afterward — perhaps on the first day the games were given — beneath the purple awning of the Colosseum, a monk from Asia Minor named Telemachus leaped down into the arena and, while he struggled to part the duelists, was stoned to death by the indignant crowd. At that point, Honorius decided that he must take decisive action. Five years earlier he had abolished the gladiatorial schools. In 404, he abolished the games themselves, though criminals were still condemned to fight against wild beasts in the arena for at least another hundred years.

Many conservative Romans, in addition to Symmachus, deplored the passing of the games, which they looked upon both as a national school of courage and as an important social link between the ruler and his subjects. The games were a part of the Roman system, and once Honorius had prohibited the sport, traditionally minded citizens must have expected that some dire event would follow. Nor were they wrong. In 410, the Eternal City, which (cried Saint Jerome from his monastery) "had taken captive all the world," was entered and sacked by Alaric, the king of the Visigoths.

Meanwhile Symmachus himself had died; the pagan aristocracy to which he belonged was slowly abandoning its proud resistance to Christianity. But once Rome had succumbed to an invader, Christian and pagan alike felt that they confronted universal ruin. Jerome, who was both a Christian ascetic and a learned classical scholar — and who numbered among his correspondents some of the most exalted members of the Roman aristocracy — wrote that his "soul shuddered" and he was "choked with sobs" when he surveyed the present crisis. The sack of Rome was a far more appalling tragedy than the fire and slaughter that had recently overwhelmed half a dozen great provincial towns.

Alaric's occupation of Rome, however, lasted only three days; according to modern historians, he did comparatively little damage to the framework of the city. His resentment against the empire was tempered with deep respect. Although he had embraced the Arian heresy (which taught that Jesus was neither all man nor all God), he was himself a pious Christian, and he had once served under the standard of the Emperor Theodosius as a commander of guerrilla troops. Alaric's object was less to humiliate Rome than to feed his hungry tribesmen and to claim for the Visigoths the share he felt they deserved in the abundant Roman way of life. Not until he had been repeatedly frustrated by imperial politicians did he launch an attack upon the empire. He entered Italy in the year 400, after first invading and plundering Greece. Then, when negotiations with the imperial court — which had abandoned its headquarters at Milan and taken refuge among the marshlands of Ravenna — proved fruitless, Alaric led his army down the road to Rome.

Twice Alaric was bought off as he stood at the gates of the city. His third blockade was more decisive. On August 24, 410, his army burst into the streets of Rome. Gibbon sums up the catastrophe in a particularly resounding paragraph:

The King of the Goths, who no longer dissembled his appetite for plunder and revenge, appeared in arms under the walls of the capital; and the trembling senate . . . prepared, by a desperate resistance, to delay the ruin of their country. But they were unable to guard against the secret conspiracy of their slaves and domestics. . . . At the hour of midnight, the Salarian gate was silently opened, and the inhabitants were awakened by the tremendous sound of the Gothic trumpet. Eleven hundred and sixty-three years after the foundation of Rome, the imperial city, which had subdued and civilized so considerable a portion of mankind, was delivered to the licentious fury of the tribes of Germany and Scythia.

In fact, Alaric's treatment of Rome was surprisingly merciful by Roman standards. It compared favorably, for example, with the behavior of the Emperor Titus when he had pillaged and destroyed Jerusalem in the year 70. The Visigoth leader is said to have ordered his men to refrain from killing and raping and to content themselves with plundering.

Not all of the members of the barbarian horde obeyed Alaric, but contrary to the custom of every previous war, writes Saint Augustine, they at least "spared those who fled to holy places out of reverence for the name of Christ." At the same time, the Visigoths secured the saint's approval by violating the pagan sanctuaries: "They attacked in the name of Christ the . . . demons and rites of unholy sacrifice . . . with such vigor that they seemed to be waging a far more bitter war with gods than with men."

Yet Roman citizens were certainly tortured and murdered by Alaric's men; and some famous monuments, including the venerable Palace of Sallust, are known to have gone up in flames. Meanwhile the invaders accumulated an enormous store of precious booty, which they heaped into the lumbering wagon train that always accompanied a barbarian army. Otherwise, much of the destruction they caused was, no doubt, largely accidental. The Visigoths were admirers as well as conquerors; and one of the most remarkable bands of tourists ever to wander around the Colosseum must have been these bellicose migrants — tall, shock-headed men from the northern forests and steppes whose elders, we are told, wore the skins of wild beasts and whose young warriors, carrying spears and battle-axes, displayed short green tunics edged with purple.

When they abandoned Rome after three days of plundering, they left it — though greatly impoverished — at first sight almost unscarred. Indeed, there were some observers to whom the city now seemed doubly gay and beautiful. To Claudius Rutilius Namatianus, a gifted pagan poet of Gallic descent who paid his tribute to Rome just three years later, the city he had always loved at a distance was still the "fair queen of the world, mother of men and mother of gods." The ancient temples on the Capitoline Hill had not yet lost their burnished golden roofs; and one of the poet's last impressions, as he finally said good-by, was the sound of distant cheering from the Circus Maximus. Having returned to Gaul, Rutilius found that the Visigoth armies had destroyed his home and overrun his lands. But like his

Christian contemporary Orosius, the Spanish collaborator of Saint Augustine, Rutilius thought that no Roman citizen need ever feel that he was really homeless. His homeland extended throughout Europe; wherever he traveled, he came "as a Roman among Romans."

Once it had passed through the crisis of the Visigoth invasion, Rome regained its old ascendancy. The city that had ceased to rule the world continued to dominate its imagination. Then a far more serious menace appeared. The Vandals, Tacitus had written three centuries earlier, were the most formidable of the German tribes. When they attacked after dark, as they were always fond of doing, they blackened their faces and their shields alike, and "this novel and, as it were, hellish apparition" often terrorized their Roman enemies. Since Tacitus's day, the Vandals had ventured far afield, subjugating Spain and seizing the ports of North Africa, from which they conducted a series of destructive raids along the Mediterranean coastline.

In 455 the Vandal chieftain Genseric landed on Italian soil, seized Rome without difficulty, and pillaged the metropolis for two weeks. The Vandals were considerably more destructive and far more brutal than the Visigoths had been. The Temple of Capitoline Jupiter lost the golden roof that Rutilius had so much admired, and when Genseric finally sailed away, amid the valuable objects heaped into the ships at Ostia were the seven-branched candelabra and other sacred Jewish vessels that Titus had removed from the Temple at Jerusalem.

Yet once again Rome survived the blow and recovered something of its former majesty. Visiting the city in 467 upon his appointment as governor of Rome, Apollinaris Sidonius, the cultivated bishop of the Auvergne and a well-known poet of his day, describes it as a busy, festive place and speaks of the holiday crowd that filled the circus and the markets. In the fashionable quarters of the city, great noblemen continued to keep open house. Displays of oratory and literary recitations still attracted large gatherings.

Very different, alas, was the social life in the former Roman provinces. At home in Gaul, Sidonius found it necessary to pay court to the local Visigoth sovereigns, King Euric and Queen Ragnahilda, and attend their rude festivities. Western Europe had at length been broken up into a network of barbarian kingdoms; and in the year 476 Romulus Augustulus, last of the Roman emperors in the West, was quietly swept aside by Odoacer, a barbarian warlord. Yet even then, during the closing days of the empire, as their world collapsed around them, the Romans would appear to have retained a sense of their own invincible superiority.

The decay of the city itself was, no doubt, a very gradual process. Both Saint Augustine and Saint Jerome had exulted over the fall of the ancient gods and goddesses — whose existence they did not deny, but whom they regarded as malevolent demons. Although Saint Jerome had declared that the temples on the Capitoline Hill were "dusty and neglected," outwardly they had not lost their grandeur. Since Theodosius had prohibited pagan worship in 392, a succession of rulers had done their best to check the destructive fury of the Christians. In the East, bands of savage enthusiasts led by fanatical monks had ruined many famous pagan sanctuaries, but in Rome Theodosius had urged the Senate to protect the masterpieces of ancient sculpture.

Imperial Rome had always been full of statues. At

the beginning of the fifth century, during the reign of Honorius, the city contained 2 *colossi,* over 20 large equestrian effigies, and more than 150 important statues of the gods, some of them gilded bronze and some of ivory. They were far less numerous than the statues of emperors and distinguished citizens that populated every public place, and they were cared for by an officer known as the *curator statuarum,* who was under the jurisdiction of the urban prefect.

Early in the sixth century, even barbarian rulers thought these statues worth protecting. As self-styled King of the Ostrogoths and Romans, *Gothorum Romanorumque Rex,* Theodoric the Great was anxious to restore the forms and usages of ancient Rome; he was also much concerned about the welfare of its bronze and marble population, which, he remarked, was nearly "equal to its natural one." Theodoric went so far as to order his officer, the Count of Rome, to establish nightly patrols and bid them exercise the keenest vigilance. While bolts and bars, he wrote, could not secure a house from robbery, "much more do the precious things left in the streets and open spaces of Rome require protection. I refer to that most abundant population of statues, to that mighty herd of horses which adorn our city. It is true that if there were any reverence in human nature, it . . . ought to be sufficient guardian of the beauty of Rome." But the times were bad, and robbers numerous. "Do you and your staff and the soldiers at your disposal watch especially by night. . . . At night the theft looks tempting; but the rascal who tries it is easily caught if the guardian approaches him unperceived." Threatened with the loss of an arm or a leg, the work of art itself might find a voice. "Nor are the

statues absolutely dumb; the ringing sound which they give forth under the blows of the thief" seemed intended to awake the drowsy watchman.

Theodoric's successor, Theodatus, continued to have the Roman statues guarded. In a letter to the urban prefect he laments that the brazen elephants on the Sacred Way had been allowed to fall into decay. It was much to be regretted, he observed, that "whereas these animals live in the flesh a thousand years, their brazen effigies should be so soon crumbling away. See, therefore, that their gaping limbs be strengthened with iron hooks, and that their drooping bellies be fortified by masonry placed underneath them."

Despite these precautions, thefts continued. Bronze was a costly metal, and marble could be burned for lime. Yet when Belisarius reconquered Rome for the Eastern Empire in 536, he found 3,785 statues still standing. Similarly, the architectural monuments of Rome — notwithstanding Christian assaults and barbarian inroads — had a very long existence, though in times of emergency their golden ornaments had been removed and melted down. However, no attacks had yet been made upon the fabric of the Colosseum; the only harm that it suffered seems to have been done by earthquakes. It was severely damaged — first in 422, after which the emperors Theodosius II and Valentinian III carefully repaired the building (additional repairs were made in 467 and 472), and again in 508, thirty-two years after the deposition of Romulus Augustulus, when Italy had become a Gothic kingdom.

Unlike the Flavian Amphitheater, the imperial residences on the Palatine Hill slowly sank into decrepitude. A huge cliff of marble-faced structures looking out across the Sacred Way, the Palatium had again and again been enlarged as successive occupants pushed out platforms and buttresses that often submerged their predecessors' work. The result was a complex mass of masonry, incorporating the Augustan Palace, the Palace of Tiberius, and the stately structure raised by Domitian when he abandoned Nero's Golden House. A labyrinth of courtyards and colonnades, of throne rooms and banqueting halls and closed gardens — for example, the famous Gardens of Adonis that Domitian had laid out on an elaborate oriental pattern — the Palatium was a self-contained city. Among its buildings — in addition to a number of temples dedicated to Cybele, Mother of the Gods, Jupiter, Minerva, and the Divine Augustus — were two libraries, Latin and Greek, and the Paedogogium, school of the imperial pages. There, on a wall of the Paedogogium, a nineteenth-century archaeologist discovered a caricature of the crucified Christ, represented with an ass's head, and above it the inscription in Greek "Alexamenos worships his God" — evidently scratched into the wall by some scornful young unbeliever to ridicule a fellow page's creed.

In 455, Genseric's Vandals had invaded and looted the imperial palace. But later in the fifth century and halfway through the sixth century, two foreign governors, King Theodoric, a Goth, and the eunuch Narses, a Byzantine, had reoccupied the apartments of the Caesars and set about restoring them. Theodoric decreed that two hundred pounds of gold, proceeds of the wine tax, should be devoted to the preservation of these apartments. Narses, accompanied by four hundred attendants, held an impressive court upon the Palatine. But although some buildings were still in good repair,

others were collapsing into total ruin. No one could arrest their rapid decay. Soon a wilderness of overgrown chambers, crumbling walls, and broken columns, riddled with dark crevices leading to subterranean depths, formed an impenetrable barrier across the hill between its eastern and its western verges.

Throughout the Dark Ages, which were then enveloping Rome, the Colosseum was among the few monuments that preserved their look of pagan dignity, neither half-demolished by long abuse and neglect nor summarily reconstructed to serve a Christian purpose. Cassiodorus, the capable Roman official whom Theodoric had appointed as his Latin secretary, tells us that in his day the Flavian Amphitheater continued to draw enormous crowds. The gladiatorial games were, of course, extinct. What this audience had come to see were wrestling matches and the familiar wild beast shows. Writing on behalf of his Gothic master to the Consul Maximus in 523, Cassiodorus expresses his disapproval. If singers and dancers were to receive a reward so, he supposes, should "the *Venator,* the fighter with wild beasts in the amphitheater . . . for *his* endeavors to please the people, who, after all, are secretly hoping to see him killed. And what a horrible death he dies — denied even the rites of burial, disappearing before he has yet become a corpse into the maw of the hungry animal he has failed to kill!"

Cassiodorus then gives a lurid but, owing to the obscurity of his barbaric prose style, a somewhat confusing account of the performances he himself had witnessed in the Colosseum. One *bestiarius,* armed only with a wooden lance, creeps toward the animal on knees or belly. Another performs a kind of crazy dance, spring-

The Vandal warriors who virtually leveled the imperial city in 455 had conquered Roman North Africa some fifteen years earlier. Settling among the local population, they established huge estates and grand villas. By the early sixth century, when this mosaic was created, a prosperous Vandal landowner had little in common with his rapacious fellow barbarians.

ing wildly into the air to avoid the beast's attack. Again, the animal fighter advances across the arena "like a hedgehog," behind a protective screen of reeds. Or he may be attached to a huge revolving wheel, which alternately swings him within the animal's grasp and lifts him high above its claws. "There are as many perilous forms of encounter as Vergil described varieties of crime and punishment in Tartarus. Alas for the pitiable error of mankind! If they had any true intuition of Justice, they would sacrifice as much wealth for the preservation of human life as now they lavish on its destruction."

Such were the spectacles that the Colosseum provided at the beginning of the sixth century. Toward the end of the century, the amphitheater is said to have been already overgrown with grass. As the Goths contended with the Byzantines, and the Lombards, another belligerent Germanic people, moved down from the hostile north, a succession of disasters befell the city itself, leaving it ruinous and half-deserted. When Totila, last of the great Ostrogothic chieftains, recaptured Rome in 546, he found (according to the Byzantine historian Procopius) only five hundred inhabitants still alive. During his stay, Totila burned the Trasteverine district, demolished a large part of the famous Aurelian Walls, and threatened to convert the whole city into "a pasture for cattle."

Totila's Byzantine adversary, Belisarius, pleaded with him to spare its ancient monuments:

> Beyond all cities on earth Rome is the greatest and most wonderful. For neither has she been built by the energy of a single man, nor has she attained to such greatness and beauty in a short time. On the contrary, a long succession of emperors, many associations of illustrious men, countless years and wealth . . . have been required to bring together all the treasures she contains . . . she remains a monument of the virtues of the world . . . and a trespass against her greatness would justly be regarded as an outrage. . . . Since things are so, admit that one of two things must necessarily happen. In this war thou must either be defeated by the Emperor, or thou must subdue him, if that be possible. Art thou victor? Destroying Rome, thou wilt lose not the city of another but thine own. Preserving her . . . thou wilt enrich thyself with the most splendid possessions of the earth.

Totila, like Alaric before him, had no real desire to lay waste the city, but his three sieges and the havoc and misery they caused its citizens certainly helped to complete its final degradation.

Natural calamities also played a part in the decline of the city. Later in the sixth century, a disastrous flood of the Tiber, which swept away many ancient buildings, was followed by a fearful plague. Signs and portents, numerous at every period of Roman history, made the visitation of plague all the more terrible; men saw death-dealing angels hovering above the roofs and heard the sound of mysterious trumpets booming out across the sky.

In the year 590, as a desperate last resort, the entire populace under the leadership of the pope himself formed a long procession of penitents that slowly moved through the deserted streets. Some penitents, already plague-stricken, dropped from the procession and were left behind for dead. But when the marchers reached the Mausoleum of Hadrian, now the Castel Sant'Angelo, the Archangel Michael is said to have appeared in the heavens and signified the end of the pestilence by sheathing the fiery sword he carried.

The procession of 590, writes the nineteenth-century German historian Ferdinand Gregorovius, "may be regarded as the beginning of Rome's Middle Ages." The man who led the penitents, the saintly Pope Gregory I, was the product of a rich patrician family, who before he adopted the monastic life had "paraded the city in splendid silken raiment." Gregory, however, was a typical early medieval Christian, learned but simply and deeply pious, a stern critic of the ancient pagan world and its surviving art and literature. The study of the old poets he dismissed as "foolishness"; the man who praised Jupiter, he announced, was not fit to praise Christ. Above all else, Pope Gregory longed to save souls; and it was he who, in 596, touched by the sight of a youthful group of fair-haired slaves, sent out his missionaries from Rome to proselytize the savage Britons. Meanwhile, his distrust of ancient learning made him the archenemy not only of grammar and syntax but also of the works of art that Alaric had spared and Theodoric had done his best to save. Smug medieval chroniclers like to credit the pope with many acts of Christian vandalism, describing how he had knocked off the heads and disfigured the limbs of unnumbered gods and goddesses and cast their statues into the Tiber.

Yet Gregory protected the interests of his flock, and he fought a long battle to restore the aqueducts that gave the city running water. Deprived of its aqueducts, Rome was bound to perish, but none of Gregory's entreaties could persuade the Count of the Aqueducts, a dilatory Byzantine bureaucrat, to clear their sluices or restore their crumbling arches. Rome, Gregory cried, was now a broken vessel; the Roman state he compared to an aged eagle, dying in its ruined eyrie. There were ruins everywhere. Now that they had lost their water supply, the great imperial baths were vacant shells. Fountains had ceased to flow, and the magnificent market places that had impressed Constantius II were fast becoming rubbish heaps.

Gregory died in the year 604. In the summer of 663 the Emperor Constans II arrived from Constantinople on a visit to another pope, Vitalian. Like his distant predecessor Constantius II, the Byzantine emperor surveyed the ancient capital, though, it is clear, with very different feelings.

He, too, ascended the Palatine Hill, where, amid the debris of the old Palatium, he and his courtiers found some habitable rooms. But three centuries had passed since the visit of Constantius II. The pagan sanctuaries that had astonished the emperor then were now roofless and deserted, and grass was beginning to grow on the tiers of the silent Colosseum. Although he could not admire the city, Constans decided that it was worth plundering. He stayed there only twelve days, but during that time he arranged for the removal of almost all Rome's noblest bronzes, and simultaneously he stripped the precious gilded tiles from the roof of the Pantheon. These treasures Constans carried off to Syracuse, in Sicily, where he spent some four years. Soon after his murder — he was killed in his bath by a slave — the Saracens invaded Sicily, and the works of art he had collected were destroyed or sold and melted down.

Constans had dealt Rome a final blow. All that remained of its ancient pagan spirit had, at last, been snuffed out.

V

POETS, POPES AND PATRIOTS

In its last agonies the Roman Empire was still capable of inspiring reverence, and even its death could not quite destroy the aura that had so long surrounded the imperial city. There Charlemagne, the King of the Franks who dreamed of reviving the great Caesarean tradition, chose to be crowned Holy Roman Emperor on Christmas Day of the year 800. And once he had been acclaimed by the crowd that filled St. Peter's Basilica, Pope Leo III, we are told, "worshiped Charles according to the manner of the ancient princes."

Rome by then was also the heart of the Christian universe. As the ultimate *refugium peccatorum,* or refuge of the contrite sinner, it had now begun to attract an unending stream of pilgrims. Some were illiterate zealots, dusty and travel-worn; others found time to examine the city and admire its pagan splendors. And every educated traveler gazed with astonishment at the tremendous Colosseum. Travelers' tales describing the amphitheater had been carried far across Europe until eventually they had even reached the monastery on the desolate northeastern shore of Britain where the Venerable Bede had passed his adult life.

Bede, who died in 735, was the most erudite man of his day; learning, teaching, and writing, he said, had always been his keenest joys. What he learned of Rome, probably from German pilgrims, convinced him that the gigantic arena must be the symbol of Rome's strength and greatness, bound up not only with the future of Rome but with the whole of human history. *"Quamdiu stabit Colysaeus,"* he prophesied, *"stabit et Roma: Quando cadet Colysaeus, cadet et Roma: Quando cadet Roma, cadet et Mundus"* — words that, more than a thousand years later, Byron was to translate in his poetic travel picture *Childe Harold:*

> While stands the Coliseum, Rome shall stand
> When falls the Coliseum, Rome shall fall,
> And when Rome falls — the world.

Medieval man was deeply attached to the marvelous. In the view of then-current authorities, the earth itself formed a roughly circular expanse, encompassed by the streams of Ocean and roofed over by a nest of crystalline spheres, with the moon, the planets, and the stars set like jewels on their shining surface. And every region of the earth had its own marvels and prodigies and grotesque, misshapen creatures. Asia, for example, was the home of the *skiapods,* men who had only one foot — though that foot was so large they could raise it above their heads to shelter them against the sun — and of the *phanesii,* men whose enormous drooping ears could be wrapped comfortably around their ribs. No less remarkable were many of the supposed denizens of Africa, and Europe itself could claim some curious inhabitants: the mermaids that bobbed off the coasts of Greece; the *ostricius,* a species of ostrich that had the head of a goose, the body of a crane, and the feet of a calf; and the *cynocephali,* the dog-headed men who were said to roam the wilder parts of Norway.

In the Middle Ages maps were eagerly studied both by scholars and by sovereigns. Charlemagne, a keen collector of maps, had acquired a panoramic view of Rome inscribed on the surface of a silver table, which is said to have afforded him the greatest pleasure. Besides depicting legendary beasts and birds and the savage peoples among whom they lived, the medieval mapmaker naturally included a scattering of famous cities. In the Hereford World Map, the masterpiece of a monkish scribe attached to an English cathedral about the year 1300, we find a sketch of Rome, with the explanatory line *"Roma caput mundi tenet orbis frena rotundi"* (Rome, the head of the world, holds the round world's guiding reins).

By that time the most popular guidebook to Rome, the *Mirabilia Romae,* or *Marvels of Rome,* written about the middle of the twelfth century, had already been completed for the use of pilgrims. The book ran through several editions, and a later version gives an extended, if fanciful, account of the glories of the Flavian Amphitheater:

> The Colosseum was the temple of the Sun, of marvellous greatness and beauty, disposed with many diverse vaulted chambers, and all covered with an heaven of gilded brass, where thunders and lightenings and glittering fires were made, and where rain was shed through slender tubes. Besides this there were the Signs super-celestial and the planets *Sol* and *Luna* . . . drawn along in their proper chariots.

The other antiquities of Rome are described by the medieval author in a profoundly reverential spirit:

> These and many more temples and palaces of emperors, consuls, senators, and prefects were in the time of the heathen within this Roman city, even as we have read in old chronicles, and have seen with our eyes, and have heard tell of ancient men. And moreover, how great was their beauty in gold, and silver, and brass, and ivory, and precious stones, we have endeavoured . . . as well as we could, to bring back to the remembrance of mankind.

As a modern historian has pointed out, the *Mirabilia* appeared at an opportune moment. Rome had recently recovered from a particularly brutal sack — this time

ROMA

by the Normans — and a revived version of the Roman Senate had just proclaimed a new republic. Earlier, in 846, a Saracen army, which apparently failed to penetrate the heart of Rome, had plundered the Vatican and St. Peter's Basilica, where it had broken into the tomb of the apostle and carried off the high altar. But the ninth-century Saracen raid could not be compared with the ferocious onslaught of the Norman armies two hundred years later.

In 1084 Pope Gregory VII, anxious to expel the Emperor Henry IV and the antipope, Clement III, who had usurped his sacred throne, was unwise enough to invoke the help of Robert Guiscard, the Norman soldier of fortune. Guiscard stormed and entered Rome on May 28, 1084. But having rescued Gregory from the Castel Sant'Angelo, where the pope had been obliged to take shelter, Guiscard was suddenly attacked by the Romans. In retaliation he plundered and burned the city and sold many of its inhabitants into slavery. Guiscard did not retire until a deputation of citizens had prostrated themselves before his feet.

At the beginning of the next century, Rome was still scarred by the Norman sack. What remained of the buildings on the Capitoline and Palatine hills had received particularly savage treatment. A number of ancient porticoes had at last collapsed in ruin, the districts surrounding the Colosseum and the Lateran had been completely burned out, and it is thought that the Colosseum itself and the triumphal arches of the Sacred Way were not allowed to go undamaged. Once more Rome, the former "head of the world," seemed to have sunk beyond recall. When the poetic Bishop Hildebert of Tours surveyed its ruins about 1106, he composed

two Latin lamentations, the second supposed to be delivered by the genius of "the widowed city":

> When I still took pleasure in idols, my army, my people, and my marble magnificence were my pride. The idols and palaces are fallen; people and Knights have sunk into servitude, and Rome scarcely remembers Rome. . . .

Throughout the Middle Ages poets continued to grieve over the degradation of the city. Dante pictured it as a "desolate widow," weeping for the emperor, its faithless master, and Petrarch, as a gray-haired matron, her garments torn, "her face overspread with the pallor of misery . . . yet with an unbroken spirit. . . ." Enough remained of the ancient city, however, to stir a literary imagination, and the twelfth-century *Mirabilia Romae* was followed by a series of books composed on much the same principle.

Rome also excited the minds of artists. The first medieval drawing of the city, executed between 1320 and 1328, presents the customary panoramic view. The Colosseum has the lofty dome described in the pages of the *Mirabilia*; indeed, the dome reappears in a fifteenth-century manuscript of Uberti's *Dittamondo*, in which Rome is depicted as an aged, black-garbed woman who sits and mourns beside the Tiber. Slightly less inaccurate are the Golden Seal of the Emperor Ludwig of Bavaria engraved in 1328, the engaging circular picture that Taddeo di Bartolo painted for the chapel of the municipal palace at Siena about 1414, and the circular vignette that Pol de Limbourg, working from 1412 to 1416, decided to slip into the decorative background of the *Très Riches Heures* of the Duc de Berry. Each portrays a roofless Colosseum, with the other marvels of Rome summarily grouped around it.

Taddeo di Bartolo, whose view is the most complex, finds room for more than seventy monuments — including the Pantheon, the Theater of Marcellus, Hadrian's Tomb (Castel Sant'Angelo), the equestrian statue of Marcus Aurelius (now on the Capitoline in the Piazza del Campidoglio), and the marble horses on the Quirinal Hill.

Among these famous edifices, in Taddeo di Bartolo's scene, rises an occasional tower, one of the rugged strong points that had sprung up in the Middle Ages. The city had by then become the battleground of aggressive feudal clans, every clan occupying a separate stronghold, from which it waged unceasing war against its neighbors. So completely had the Romans forgotten their past that they treated its ruins as convenient quarries. Besides burning marble statues for lime and selling cut stone and polished antique columns to the builders of the new cathedrals, they would often wrench out entire blocks of masonry for use in modern keeps and palaces.

Soon the Roman horizon bristled with towers, often planted on some crumbling monument. "Not a single triumphal arch," writes the nineteenth-century historian Gregorovius, "remained unsurmounted by a tower." The Frangipani, a family that had begun to make its mark some 150 years earlier, had seized the arches of Titus and Constantine about the twelfth century, and turned them into massive donjons. In 1144 they fortified the Circus Maximus, and in the same year Pope Lucius II allowed them to occupy the Colosseum, which itself became a fortress. Meanwhile, among the ruins of the ancient Capitol, the powerful Colonnas lived like robber barons.

Later the Frangipani were expelled from the Colosseum by a family named Annibaldi, who supported the Colonna faction. And in March 1337 among the guests they received at the Colosseum was the great lyric poet Petrarch, then a man of thirty-two, who was visiting the city for the first time. Although he had been born at Arezzo, the son of a Florentine notary, Petrarch had spent much of his youth at Avignon. Since 1309 — when a French pontiff, elected by French cardinals, had turned his back upon the Vatican — Avignon had been the official residence of the popes.

It was in Provence that the young Italian poet had encountered his beloved Laura. She was a virtuous young married woman — probably the wife of a local grandee, Hugues de Sade — around whose person Petrarch had proceeded to build up a visionary and romantic cult, like Dante's famous cult of Beatrice. Although during the course of the poet's long attachment to her Laura bore her husband several children — while he himself produced two bastard offspring — Petrarch's passion ended only with her death.

The poet, in 1337, was visiting Rome as the guest of the Colonna family. Cardinal Giovanni Colonna had become his literary patron, and the cardinal's younger brother, Bishop Giacomo Colonna — "that incomparable man," he wrote, "serious, eager, wise, virtuous" — was the greatest friend Petrarch ever made. At the family stronghold he was entertained by their father, the noble patriarch Stefano Colonna, and met the cardinal's uncle, a devout and learned personage, who escorted him around the city. Petrarch immediately lost his heart to Rome. The guidebook he had brought with him was the celebrated *Mirabilia Romae,* but

Petrarch was probably the first tourist to see Rome from a more imaginative point of view — not as a collection of legendary marvels but as a moving record of the human past that spoke to him in a language he understood, of experiences he might himself perhaps have shared.

Sometimes he would scale the mountainous ruins of the Baths of Diocletian, breathe in the atmosphere of space and solitude, and contemplate the scene below. Fourteenth-century Rome presented a gloomy prospect — cows pastured across the Sacred Way and houses, taverns, and workshops clustered around the Colosseum. But for a perceptive eye, the past was everywhere. Often a vinedresser would approach the poet "with a gem of ancient workmanship or a gold or silver coin in his hand, turned up by his mattock, to sell it or ask me if I could recognize the engraved face of some hero."

That summer Petrarch returned to Avignon, but he paid Rome a second and more important visit during the spring of 1341. Since his first visit, he had decided to have himself crowned as poet laureate on no less a place than the sacred Capitoline Hill. After a great deal of cautious maneuvering, he had managed to procure an invitation. The idea was symbolic: Laura's visionary lover would receive a wreath of laurel leaves. It was also practical: Petrarch could now stand forth as the poetic spokesman of the fallen city. His chief supporter was King Robert of Naples, a pious and extremely cultivated monarch. Before entering Rome, the poet spent a month at Naples, where Robert wrapped his own robe around Petrarch's shoulders. A king among poets, he was now prepared to accept his laurel crown wearing truly royal raiment.

Another symbolic touch: Petrarch arrived in Rome on Good Friday, April 6, 1341, the fourteenth anniversary of his first encounter with Laura at the church of St. Clare in Avignon. He was crowned on Easter Sunday, and wearing King Robert's robe, he delivered an eloquent speech that lasted for some thirty minutes. He spoke on the art of poetry, which differed, he said, from the other arts because it could not be acquired simply by toil and intellectual diligence but demanded "a kind of inner power," divinely infused throughout the artist's spirit. It was "a sweet love" that drew him toward "the lonely, difficult slopes of Parnassus." Mere study, "without love and without a certain delight and gusto of the mind," would never bring him to his goal. At the same time, he uttered a fervent prayer: "Long live the Roman people — and God maintain them in liberty!"

Before the month had ended, Petrarch left Rome. The next year he was back in Provence, enjoying the delicious quietude of his little house near the romantic Fontaine de Vaucluse. A year later he was again reminded of Rome, when a Roman delegation arrived in Avignon on a diplomatic errand to the papal court. In their train came the bold young enthusiast Cola di Rienzi, or Rienzo, who represented a small religious and political society. They styled themselves "The Thirteen Good Men," but Cola immediately began to outshine and outtalk his fellow delegates. The offspring of a laundress and a tavern-keeper, Cola was not yet thirty years old. He fascinated Petrarch, for besides being a fiery patriot, a deep scholar, and a fervent lover of antiquity, he possessed an extraordinary physical charm, a melodious voice, and brilliant, piercing eyes.

Soon after their first meeting Petrarch recorded his impressions of Cola's swift, compulsive monologue. He felt that the voice he heard came from a god, not from a man. "You described to me the present decadence and destruction of the divine Republic. . . . You probed our wounds to the quick, so that the sound of your words, still ringing in my ears, brings renewed pain to my mind, tears again welling from my eyes, flames bursting from my heart."

Cola's theme was the agony of Rome and the misdeeds of its modern nobles. Many of those vilified nobles — including, of course, the Colonnas — happened to be the poet's friends. But when Cola was accused of holding heretical views, Petrarch wrote on his behalf to Cardinal Colonna, who good-naturedly persuaded the pope to forgive him and even to provide the alleged heretic with a modest official salary.

Later, when Cola had regained Rome, Petrarch heard the story of his friend's new adventure. Cola had boldly declared war against the Roman noble families, proclaiming them to be tyrants and bloodsuckers. By way of reply one of the Colonna henchmen had struck the young man in the face. Meanwhile Cola advertised his championship of the people with huge cartoons that were carried through the streets and by the inflammatory slogans that he plastered on public buildings. *"In breve tempo,"* read the interested crowd, *"gli Romani torneranno al loro antico buono stato"* (In a short time the Romans will return to their ancient good estate). Finally Cola felt that the moment had come to transform propagandist agitations into downright revolutionary action. He chose the Feast of Pentecost, in May 1347, during Stefano Colonna's temporary absence from the city. That morning, fully armored except that he wore no helmet — beneath a banner that bore the proud legend *"Roma caput mundi"* (Rome, head of the world), two additional papal banners that showed his peaceful aims, and the blood-red flag of freedom — Cola ascended to the Capitol. There he announced the liberation of "the sacred Roman republic."

Cola di Rienzi has been called "the first of liberators, first architect of modern democracy." These claims may not be exaggerated, but Cola, like Petrarch, had a foot in two entirely different worlds — in the Middle Ages, to which he belonged by tradition, and in the springtime world of the Renaissance. Petrarch, too, though he had many medieval traits — his profound religious faith and the strain of asceticism that, once Laura had died, would cause him to reject the pleasures of the flesh and "the obscene act" of love — often anticipated the Renaissance poets and essayists. Some of his dicta recall the opinions of Montaigne. "Livers of busy lives," Petrarch had decided, "do not live. They talk with others, not with themselves." Elsewhere, he recommended following one's own nature, which understands what we are and what is good for us. Cato had said that the best guide is nature. So Petrarch had always submitted to nature, and had determined that he always would, unless — a typically medieval provision — the Almighty had commanded otherwise.

Reports of Cola's bloodless coup, when they reached Avignon, caused the poet keen delight. At last Rome, of which he had written with such deep nostalgic feeling, would again be truly free:

L'antiche mura che ancor teme e ama
E trema il mondo quando si remembra
Del tempo andato . . .

Those ancient walls on which, when it remembers past days, the world still looks with fear and love and trembling . . .

And despite his former friendship with the Colonnas, whose haughty towers and palaces Cola now proposed to confiscate, Petrarch poured out a flood of indignation against unworthy Roman nobles. Cola, he cried, was a second Brutus. Not only had his enemies robbed the people, they had plundered the ruins of the ancient city: "They even wreaked their vengeance on ancient marbles! They have broken down the triumphal arches and sold the stones . . . you Romans have done nothing! You were sheep! But now you are awake. Drive out the ravening wolves! . . . Do you, O Tribune, rush to combat!"

The new tribune needed no encouragement — he had always loved a battle. But during the next few weeks, while Cola was busily reforming Rome and establishing the pattern of its future greatness, a more alarming side of his character appeared, both in his deeds and in his words. Like most Italians, ancient and modern, he had a passion for the splendid gesture; indeed, there was something about Cola of the young Benito Mussolini. His public proclamations became increasingly extravagant. Having been dubbed knight, not only did he proclaim that Rome was now the capital of the world but also, drawing his sword, he slashed through the empty air toward the east and west and north, crying *"Questo e mio!"* (This belongs to me). Similarly, when he was appointed tribune, he assumed the sumptuous regalia of a sovereign, while the references he made to Jesus Christ showed that he was beginning to regard himself as at once a heavenly and an earthly savior.

DOMINVS FRANCISCHVS PETRARCHA

It was not long before the nobles struck back. Although three of the Colonnas died during an abortive attempt to recapture the city — Cola dipped his youthful son into a roadside pool that was still reddened with their lifeblood — a real counterrevolution broke out in mid-December 1348. Cola, whose nerve had suddenly snapped, was obliged to flee from Rome. He did not return until 1354. Again attempting to seize power, he exhibited all the most unpleasant traits of a disappointed revolutionary. For eloquence he substituted craft and violence, and his efforts to revive the liberated republic proved completely unsuccessful. Cola had by then lost the support of the common people, and when they rioted and set fire to the Capitol, the fallen tribune made a dash for safety.

In the end Cola's natural vanity betrayed him. Despite the fact that he had cut off his beard and blackened his face, he had not removed his golden bracelets. Recognized and surrounded, he stood at bay for an hour on the steps that led up to the Capitoline palace, silent, with folded arms, still showing a pair of purple stockings — hose "in the baronial fashion" — beneath a heavy shepherd's cloak. At last he was hacked to death, and his corpse, like Mussolini's, was exhibited in a small piazza hanging ignominiously upside down. It was afterward dragged away to the Mausoleum of Augustus, where it was burned upon a bed of thistles.

Thus ended "the last of the Roman Tribunes," and with him the magnificent dream that Cola had once shared with Petrarch. Nearly a quarter of a century passed before the popes at Avignon escaped from what Petrarch had called their "Babylonian captivity" when, in 1377, Gregory XI definitely returned to Rome.

Three years earlier Petrarch had died, but as an aging man he continued to think of Rome and to implore the pope to leave Avignon: "Rome needs her spouse! The Lateran is falling in ruins; the mother church of the world has a rotten roof; the houses of Peter and Paul and the Holy Apostles are tottering!" Meanwhile, His Holiness should compel the emperor in Constantinople to join him in the Sacred City. Together they must defend Europe against the fast-advancing Turkish hordes.

Petrarch's vision was not to be realized, but under the papacy Rome entered a new period of political importance and religious grandeur. Some of the fifteenth-century popes were imaginative, widely cultivated men, like Pius II. Known to contemporary writers and humanists as Aeneas Sylvius, Pius II took a deep interest in the works of classical antiquity and visited many of the ancient sites. During the sixteenth century, too, both popes Alexander VI (father of Cesare and Lucrezia Borgia) and Leo X (the patron of Raphael) were devoted antiquarians. But although Leo commissioned Raphael to restore the outlines of the pagan city, the popes of this period were usually more concerned with the discovery of statues for the beautification of their own palaces than with the care of the dilapidated monuments that were crumbling all around them.

That task was left to contemporary artists and scholars. In 1431 Poggio Bracciolini had published a book, entitled *De Varietate Fortunae* (*Of the Vicissitudes of Human Fortune*), which lamented the fall of the Roman monuments — the Colosseum, he wrote, was already half-destroyed — and attempted to appraise them from a systematic point of view. In 1446 Flavio Biondo issued his *Roma Instaurata* (*Rome Restored*), which, besides enumerating the most splendid ancient structures, included some practical hints as to how they might be safeguarded. In the mind of the Renaissance man, stones were now beginning to speak with tongues. After inspecting the enormous ruins of Baiae, Boccaccio observed that they were "old walls," yet perennially "new for modern spirits." Later an Italian archaeologist, when asked why he roamed around old buildings and made careful transcripts of inscriptions, answered that his purpose was "to wake the dead."

In 1485, a strange event occurred that affected the population of the whole city. From a tomb on the Appian Way a gang of masons was said to have unearthed a sarcophagus bearing the legend "Julia, daughter of Claudius" that enclosed the body of an extraordinarily beautiful girl. She appeared to be about fifteen years old — her eyelids and mouth were half open, and her perfectly preserved limbs still had the suppleness and bloom of life. Carried to the palace on the Capitol, she drew a crowd of reverent pilgrims. "She was more beautiful," declared an eyewitness, "than can be said or written; and, were it said or written, it would not be believed by those who had not seen her." Such was the romantic devotion her body aroused that Innocent VIII, who had just succeeded to the papacy, had it removed from its shrine on the Capitol and secretly buried beyond the Pincian Gate.

Yet, notwithstanding the Renaissance cult of antiquity, temples and colonnades were still allowed to decay, and antique statues continued to be stolen and burned for lime. Among the buildings that suffered was Vespasian's Colosseum. Damaged by earthquakes

in the fifth and sixth centuries, it had again been severely shaken in 847. Then, probably during the great earthquake of 1231, the whole of its southwestern façade collapsed, reducing the noble ring of exterior arches to a shapeless pile of stones.

One of the most learned Renaissance popes was Nicholas V, a great collector of Greek manuscripts and the founder of the Vatican Library. Nevertheless, during the course of a single year, Nicholas was said to have taken more than two thousand cartloads of stone from the ruins of the amphitheater. His example was followed by Alexander VI, who leased the Colosseum, the Forum, and other monuments as commercial quarries, reserving for himself a third share of the profits. Meanwhile, treasure hunters burrowed beneath the walls of the crumbling arena, and metal thieves removed the clamps with which Vespasian's architects had linked the blocks together — hence, the ugly crevices that still scar the building's frontage. Sixteenth-century Romans liked to believe that these holes had once been made by Goths or Vandals. More probably, the damage was done by their own immediate forebears.

At any rate, when it had ceased to be the towered stronghold of the Frangipani and the Annibaldi, no one troubled to protect the Colosseum. In 1332 it is said to have been used for a bullfight, though some authorities doubt the story. From the red-draped balconies and rows of wooden seats, erected to conceal the broken tiers, Roman aristocrats applauded a procession of knights who bore on their helmets not only their lady's colors but also such devices as "I am alone like Horatius" and "I am the slave of the Roman Lucretia." These paladins fought the bulls on foot. They were

unarmored, though they carried swords and lances, and no less than eighteen heroes are supposed to have lost their lives.

After the fall of the Roman nobles, but before the popes returned from Avignon, the Colosseum was solemnly entrusted to the Roman people and their Senate. It was then handed over first to the Confraternity of the Salvatore — their sculptured coat of arms can still be seen on one of the inner arches — who acquired a third part of the building in 1381. Afterward it went to the Confraternity of the Gonfalone, another charitable organization. Its members staged an elaborate cycle of mystery plays against the background of the ruins, using some of the remaining tiers of seats and the family house that the Frangipani clan had built themselves behind the walls. In 1497 Arnold von Harff, a recently arrived German traveler, reported that he had paid a visit to "a magnificent ancient palace, called the Colosseum, round in shape, vaulted and with various orders of architecture . . . having in its center a round open space surrounded by steps which made it possible to ascend to the upper part."

In former times, Harff learned, "men sat on these steps to watch combats between gladiators and wild beasts." The spectacles he himself witnessed had been very much more edifying. "I saw there, on Holy Thursday, the Passion of Jesus Christ. Living men represented the Flagellation, the Crucifixion, the Death of Judas, and so forth. Those who took part were youths of well-to-do families, and everything was conducted with great order and decorum." But apparently the ghosts of the Colosseum, where an audience had once watched the crucifixion of the bandit Laureolus and

the slow burning alive of a criminal in the part of Hercules, must have exerted a demoralizing influence upon sixteenth-century actors. The plays, which had grown more and more profane, at length became a source of scandal, and under Pope Paul III, the patron of Michelangelo, they were finally prohibited.

Paul III had succeeded Clement VII in the year 1534. During Clement's pontificate yet another invasion by ferocious foreign troops, comparable only to Robert Guiscard's sack, had caused the Romans untold misery. In 1527 the renegade Constable of Bourbon, Duke Charles de Bourbon, commanding an imperial army made up of Germans, Spaniards, and a contingent of Italian free lances, or mercenaries, had marched against Rome with the object of deposing Clement and enthroning a pope who favored the ambitions of Emperor Charles V. At dawn on May 6 the Constable of Bourbon attacked the city's walls, and about six o'clock that morning, despite a heavy bombardment from the Castel Sant'Angelo, his troops managed to effect an entry. Meanwhile the constable himself had fallen — slain by the bullet of an harquebus as he was exhorting his men and helping them to drag up a scaling ladder.

The sack of Rome began the next day; it was one of the most horrible episodes in Roman history. "Hell," wrote an observer, "was a more beautiful thing." Many of the German soldiers, the *lanznechts* — clad in the baggy breeches, padded doublets, and fantastically feathered hats that we know from Dürer's drawings — were fierce opponents of the Catholic Church. They stabled their horses in the Vatican and in St. Peter's itself. Monks were cut down, nuns were ravished and sold into Roman brothels. The holiest relics, among them the sacred spear reputed to have pierced the side of Christ, were paraded through a jeering crowd. The imperial mercenaries gave no quarter and few of their prisoners escaped alive except by payment of a heavy ransom. Soon the streets of Rome were littered with corpses, and a plague broke out, which killed not only Romans but several important officers of the Constable of Bourbon's household.

During the first assault Pope Clement, who had been at his prayers in the Vatican, was hurried along the covered passage that led to the Castel Sant'Angelo. He was followed by his terrified cardinals, some of whom found the gates closed and had to be hauled through a window. The pope remained in the fortress until he was finally able to pay off the imperial forces. Among his attendants, none had shown greater enterprise than a young Florentine artist named Benvenuto Cellini.

That, at least, was Cellini's own account of his conduct. Cellini had never been a modest character. "In all his doings," writes the sixteenth-century art historian Giorgio Vasari, he was "of high spirit, proud, lively, very quick to act, and formidably vehement. . . ." When the imperial troops delivered their first attack, Cellini had helped defend the city walls. Seeing that one of his companions had lost his nerve and had "turned in maddest haste to fly," Cellini exclaimed that, before he himself deserted his post, he must perform some action worthy of a man. He recorded the event in his story of his own life, one of the most readable autobiographies ever written:

Directing my arquebuse where I saw the thickest and most serried troop of fighting men, I aimed exactly at one whom I remarked to be higher than the rest. . . .

Then I turned to Alessandro and Cecchino, and bade them discharge their arquebuses, showing them how to avoid being hit by the besiegers. When we had fired two rounds apiece, I crept cautiously up to the wall, and observing . . . a most extraordinary confusion, I discovered afterwards that one of our shots had killed the Constable of Bourbon; and from what I subsequently learned, he was the man whom I had first noticed above the heads of the rest.

Cellini now felt that he had justified his manhood and was entitled to join the pope at the Castel Sant'Angelo. There he again performed distinguished service, rallying the bombardiers and directing the fire of the guns, all to such good effect that he claims it was he alone who saved the fortress. Once peace had returned, Cellini resumed his position as Pope Clement's favorite jeweler, designing every kind of object from jewels and buttons to "a chalice of exceeding richness," embellished with exquisite bas-reliefs and miniature statuettes of Faith, Hope, and Charity. Besides being uncommonly vainglorious, Cellini was also wildly amorous, and in 1534 he became passionately enamored of a young Sicilian girl. He had arranged an elopement, he tells us, when her mother, "getting wind of this, left Rome secretly one night" and, taking the girl, who returned Cellini's love, hurried away toward Naples.

The artist pursued them but presently lost the scent. In his despair, which threatened to drive him to distraction, he "did a multitude of mad things." A little later when he had partly recovered his wits — and "was indulging in all the pleasures man can think of, and had engaged in another love affair, merely to drown the memory of my real passion" — he encountered a

99

Sicilian priest. Cellini had always enjoyed the conversation of the learned, and his new friend proved to be "a man of very elevated genius, well-instructed in both Greek and Latin letters." At the same time he was keenly interested in the dangerous art of necromancy, and Cellini admitted that "throughout my whole life, I have had the most intense desire to see or learn something of this art." He hoped, too, that the demons whom the necromancer conjured up might perhaps agree to reunite him with the beautiful Sicilian girl.

So Cellini agreed to "attempt the adventure." In 1534 the traditional mystery plays had just been banned from the Colosseum, and the amphitheater was then regarded as the haunt of unclean spirits. What better place for a magical ceremony? One evening the artist and the necromancer, accompanied by two likely assistants, quietly slipped into the ruins. Having donned his necromancer's robes, the Sicilian priest proceeded to trace a magic circle on the dust of the arena and then introduced his three companions. To Cellini and his comrades he entrusted the task of tending the fire he had lit and throwing into the blaze either "precious perfumes," which would attract the spirits, or "drugs of fetid odor," which, if necessary, would send them flying.

These ceremonies lasted more than an hour and a half. By that time, Cellini relates, "several legions" had appeared, and "the Colosseum was all full of devils." The priest then commanded Cellini to make some request of the assembled spirits, and Cellini called on them "to reunite me with my Sicilian Angelica." That evening the spirits gave no response, but Cellini went home well pleased. Like every Renaissance artist, he had a naturally inquisitive mind, and he had enjoyed, he

tells us, "the greatest satisfaction of my curiosity."

His second experiment was considerably more dramatic. In every magical operation, as in the Christian mass itself, an important part is played by the magician's acolyte who, the Sicilian priest instructed Cellini, should be "a little boy of pure virginity." Cellini therefore chose one of his shopboys, and with the boy, a friend named Vincenzio Romoli who had accompanied him the first time, and "a certain Agnolini Gaddi," they returned to the arena. Again the magician prepared his circle, employing "yet more wondrous ceremonies." On this occasion he commanded Vincenzio Romoli to superintend the fire and drugs:

He next placed in my hand the pentacle [a five-pointed star], when he bid me turn towards the points he indicated, and then under the pentacle I held the little boy. . . . Now the necromancer began to utter those awful invocations, calling by name on multitudes of demons who are captains of their legions, and these he summoned by the virtue and potency of God. . . . In a short space of time the whole Colosseum was full of a hundredfold as many as had appeared upon the first occasion. . . . At the advice of the necromancer, I again demanded to be reunited with Angelica. The sorcerer turned to me and said: "Hear you what they have replied; that in the space of one month you will be where she is?" Then once more he prayed me to stand firm by him, because the legions were a thousandfold more than he had summoned, and were the most dangerous of all the denizens of hell; and now that they had settled what I asked, it behoved us to be civil to them and dismiss them gently.

This, however, proved to be an extremely difficult business, and the adventurous gentlemen clustered around the brazier, with the vast outlines of the Colosseum looming darkly overhead, experienced a sudden wave of panic. As for the acolyte, he shrieked out that "a million of the fiercest men were swarming round and threatening us. He said, moreover, that four huge giants had appeared, who were striving to force their way inside the circle. Meanwhile the necromancer, trembling with fear, kept doing his best with mild and soft persuasions to dismiss them. Vincenzio Romoli . . . quaked like an aspen leaf. . . ." As for Cellini: "though I was quite as frightened as the rest of them, [I] tried to show it less, and inspired them with marvellous courage; but the truth is that I had given myself up for dead. . . ."

There was worse to come. When Cellini admonished the little boy, who was crouching with his head between his knees, and bade him boldly look up, "he cried out: 'The whole Colosseum is in flames, and the fire is advancing on us.'" Whereat Cellini ordered Agnolini Gaddi, whose eyes were starting from his head with terror, to cast a nauseous drug into the fire. At that moment Gaddi's panic fears suddenly attacked his bowels, and the horrid result proved far more effective than any of their fumigations. Hearing Cellini laugh, the little boy was again encouraged to confront the diabolic horde. He reported that they had turned tail and were now "taking to flight tempestuously." But even so, Cellini and his friends did not presume to leave the circle. They remained there beside their dying fire until they heard the matins-bell. Then, at last, the necromancer doffed his robes and packed up the great bundle of books that he had brought with him to the arena:

All together, we issued . . . from the circle, huddling as close as we could to one another, especially the boy, who had got into the middle, and taken the necromancer by his gown, and me by the cloak. All the while that we were going towards our houses . . . he kept saying that two of the devils he had seen in the Colosseum were gambolling in front of us, skipping now along the roof and now upon the ground.

Each of them, Cellini concludes, dreamed of devils all the next night, and he firmly refused the priest's suggestion that he should join him in attempting "to consecrate a book, by means of which we should extract immeasurable wealth, since we could call up friends to show us where treasures were . . . and after this wise we should become the richest of mankind." The artist felt that he had already seen enough. Once more he had proved his superior courage — and his curiosity had been fully satisfied. He had lost his taste for nocturnal adventures amid the ruins of the Colosseum.

VI

THE ROMANTIC RUIN

Like many of his distinguished contemporaries, Benvenuto Cellini was a part-time archaeologist. As a young man wandering around Rome during the intervals of work and pleasure, he always carried — besides his fowling piece, a particularly splendid weapon — a sketchbook and a pencil or a lump of beeswax. He had formed the habit, he tells us, "of going on feast-days to the ancient buildings and copying parts of them in wax or with the pencil," meanwhile shooting the rock doves — naturally, he was an excellent shot — that had found a home among the ruins. Cellini also made the acquaintance of "certain hunters after curiosities, who followed in the track of those Lombard peasants who used to come to Rome to till the vineyards," and who "frequently turned up antique medals, agates, crysoprases, cornelians, and cameos. . . ." Thus he had acquired "the head of a dolphin about as big as a good-sized ballot-bean" carved out of finely colored emerald, a cameo engraved with Hercules binding Cerberus — of which the great Michelangelo himself said that he had "never seen anything so wonderful"—and a bronze medal representing Jupiter "of the most perfect execution."

Elsewhere Cellini refers to the "arabesques . . . called grotesques by the ignorant." They had obtained this name because they were discovered in various subterranean caverns, "which caverns were formerly chambers, hot-baths, cabinets for study, halls, and apartments of like nature. The curious discovering them in such places (since the level of the ground has gradually been raised while they have remained below, and since in Rome those vaulted rooms are commonly called grottoes), it has followed that the word grotesque is applied to the patterns I have mentioned."

One of the curious who examined these underground chambers was the youthful painter Raphael. The grotesques that he and his assistant Giovanni da Udine admired early in the sixteenth century were painted on the walls of lofty corridors that had once formed part of Nero's Golden House but had been buried when the Emperor Trajan raised his baths upon the site. These designs inspired Raphael to decorate the *loggia* of the Vatican in what he believed to be the same manner.

Throughout the Renaissance, painters and architects intensively studied the Roman monuments, taking a detail here and a detail there for use in their own works. Michelangelo was among those who borrowed details from the Colosseum, and the courtyard he and Antonio da Sangallo designed for the Palazzo Farnese, with its three different superimposed orders, is a noble tribute to the ancient amphitheater. Similarly, Sangallo's designs for the new St. Peter's Basilica are described by the modern historian James Lees-Milne as "full of motives taken from the Colosseum and the Theatre of Marcellus." Roman architecture was a pattern book that all Renaissance builders used. But although it was never entirely superseded, during the next age a much more florid mode, which corresponded to the current religious revival, captured the imagination of Italian artists.

In 1545 the Council of Trent had been convened by Pope Paul III to check the inroads of Protestantism and to reform the constitution of the Catholic Church. The succeeding Counter Reformation, as it is generally called, was at first a puritanical and disciplinary movement. Among its other activities, the Council of Trent attacked the introduction of pagan subjects into contemporary religious art. Michelangelo did not escape criticism: during the 1560's, soon after the painter's death, Daniele da Volterra was commissioned to purify his *Last Judgment* by clothing the limbs of naked figures. Classical statues also aroused the resentment of the reformers, and in 1566 one of the earliest decisions of Pope Pius V was to banish all pagan statuary from the Belvedere of the Vatican.

At the opening of the next century, however, the church adopted a more indulgent attitude, and the new baroque style, already apparent in Michelangelo's later works, began to reach its final flowering. With Michelangelo, writes James Lees-Milne, architecture had "ceased to be a coldly mathematical and static science. . . . It became a dynamic force to be released from within the teeming imagination. The artist identified the physical functions of the human form with the structure he was assembling. This structure became a pullulating, sensuous thing. . . ." Naturally, less attention was paid to the solemn Roman monuments. Their mood was static; they had an unchanging dignity, whereas the inspiration of baroque architecture was organic and dramatic. There was nothing sensuous, for example, about the stately façade of the Colosseum, and between 1585 and 1590 Sixtus V commanded the architect Domenico Fontana to reconstruct the amphitheater as a textile factory. On Sixtus's death the idea was given up, but in the seventeenth century Clement IX put the ruins of the amphitheater to an equally degrading use. Barrels of saltpeter for a neighboring powder factory were stored beneath convenient arches.

Seventeenth-century Rome was a baroque city.

105

While the Colosseum lay silent and derelict, its cavernous entries barred against intruders, a host of new, splendidly ornate churches — their façades crowded with expressive angels and saints — sprang up along the Roman skyline. St. Peter's itself had by then developed wings — the vast colonnades encompassing its forecourt that Giovanni Lorenzo Bernini completed in 1666.

Born in 1598, Bernini lived to be eighty-two. During his long career he established an extraordinary record of accomplishment. His range in architecture extended from his classic colonnade for St. Peter's to the richly fantastic *baldacchino,* or decorative canopy, that he raised above Saint Peter's tomb inside the Basilica; and among his statues, from his voluptuous presentation of *The Ecstacy of St. Teresa* to the no less ecstatic group that shows Apollo chasing Daphne, who is depicted in the throes of becoming a tree, painfully burgeoning into roots and leaves. Just as accomplished are Bernini's portrait heads, which immortalize the pride and craft and vigor of a succession of seventeenth-century faces.

Bernini himself was a devout and modest character, so aware of his own artistic shortcomings that none of his masterpieces struck him as completely satisfying. When he drove through the Piazza Navona and passed the magnificent fountains he had built there, because they no longer pleased him, he would actually raise the shutters of his coach. For Bernini, his work was a fierce obsession. Often he labored seven hours at a stretch, and if an attempt were made to attract his notice he would brush it aside, exclaiming impatiently: "Do not touch me! I am in love." William Blake's maxim "Exuberance is Beauty" might well have been Bernini's watchword. The artist admired everything that was fluid and swift and forceful, violent contrasts and impassioned gestures. In some respects, he seems to have anticipated the great Romantic poets and painters of the early nineteenth century. At least he shared their dangerous love of extremes and their desire to convey through art the wildest states of human feeling.

Thanks to baroque art, Rome and its neighborhood acquired a new and unexpected beauty. For the first time, the fact that a building was ruinous made it even more impressive, and artists discovered that there was a strange romantic charm about tottering walls and broken arches. Such subjects were remarkably plentiful in the countryside of seventeenth-century Italy.

Since 1550, the Italian population had been steadily diminishing — Rome itself, by the middle of the century, had fewer than 120,000 citizens, and particularly in the Papal States and the impoverished southern provinces, there were large districts where only shepherds and bandits roamed across the sterile landscape. Around Rome stretched the Campagna a malarial plain. Once it had been covered by prosperous farms and villas, but the destruction of the Roman aqueducts — destruction that Pope Gregory I had bravely tried to prevent in the sixth century — had reduced the region to a barren waste. Nevertheless the great processions of the ruined aqueducts still marched along the tawny skyline of the Campagna and the whole surface was riddled with empty tombs and rough with outcroppings of ancient masonry.

Such was the desolation that stirred later artists. Salvator Rosa, who was born near Naples in 1615 and died in 1673, was a master of dramatic chiaroscuro. And during the eighteenth century a series of painters

The perfect symmetry of a Renaissance piazza lined with idealized Roman monuments — including an intact Colosseum — could exist only in an artist's imagination. Attributed to the fifteenth-century architect Luciano da Laurana, this romanticized vista is an early example of the science of city planning.

and draughtsmen — Giambattista Piranesi, who lived from 1720 to 1778 and executed more than two thousand engravings of the Eternal City and its monuments; Alessandro Magnasco and Giovanni Paolo Pannini; as well as many other artists of lesser note — experimented with the same themes. Together they invented an idea of "the picturesque" — a blend of wild landscape and fantastic architecture that usually included a shepherd or a group of bandits encamped amid the weeds and ruins — that at once appealed to foreign tourists. To be picturesque, a prospect had to be desolate. It was the decay of Italy, as much as its music and sunshine, that attracted inquisitive English travelers.

The English have always enjoyed travel, but not until the beginning of the Georgian Age did the Grand Tour — on which a rich young man was expected to embark once he had left his school and university — become an established social institution. English travelers of the seventeenth century were apt to be less fashionable but more learned. Several distinguished poets, including Milton, Marvell, Crashaw, and Rochester, made the journey to Rome; and a celebrated prose writer, the famous diarist John Evelyn, also explored the city.

A typical seventeenth-century polymath, Evelyn took a deep interest in almost every branch of modern knowledge, from architecture and "the natural sciences" to forestry, gardening, and book collecting. Although he had a warm heart, he clearly distrusted emotion. But his rapturous memories of Rome would remain with him until he died. Fifty years later he wrote to his traveling companion Thomas Henshaw that he frequently called to mind "the many bright and happy

moments we have passed together at Rome and other places." Whenever he thought of "the agreeable toil we took among the ruins and antiquities, to admire the superb buildings, visit the cabinets and curiosities of the virtuosi, the sweet walks by the banks of the Tiber, the Via Flaminia, the gardens and villas of that glorious city," he felt that he was young again. "The opera we saw at Venice comes into my fancy," and he was even ready to sing some verses celebrating youth and youthful happiness that had pleased them both.

Evelyn had reached Rome "on the 4th of November 1644 about 5 at night." On November 15, he tells us, having "passed through the stately Capitol" and halted to examine the Arch of Titus and the remnants of the Meta Sudans:

... we enter into the mighty ruins of the Vespatian Amphitheatre, built by that excellent Prince Titus. ... The 3 rows of Circles are yet entire. ... At the dedication of this place were 5000 wild beasts slain in 3 months during which the feast lasted to the expense of 10 millions of gold. ... It is without of a perfect Circle, and was once adorned thick with statues, remaining entire till of late that some of the stones were carried away to repair the City walls, and build the Farnesian Palace. That which still appears most admirable is the continuance of the Porticoes, vaults and stairs. ... Near it is a small chapel called Santa Maria della Pieta nel Coliseo, which is erected on the steps, or stages very lofty, at one of its sides or ranges within, and there lives only a melancholy Heremite. I ascended to the very top of it, and that with wonderful admiration.

It seems strange that a man as exact as Evelyn, afterward a celebrated member of the Royal Society, should have somehow got it into his head that the Flavian Amphitheater formed a perfect circle. An eighteenth-century traveler generally avoided mistakes by enlisting the services of a professional archaeologist, for the Grand Tour was an important part of a young man's education and he was expected to pursue his studies in a properly conscientious spirit.

With the traveler journeyed a "governor," or "bear-leader," customarily a learned parson, who arranged the itinerary, kept the domestic accounts, and was expected to protect the young man against moral dangers. The bear-leader was seldom very effective at this part of his job — a bold young roué was usually more than a match for an awkward country clergyman. In a wonderful passage that he added to the second version of *The Dunciad*, Alexander Pope depicts the fashionable dunce, a favorite protégé of the Goddess Dulness, on his triumphant way across Europe:

To where the Seine, obsequious as she runs,
Pours at great Bourbon's feet her silken sons;
Or Tiber, now no longer Roman, rolls,
Vain of Italian Arts, Italian Souls;
To happy Convents, bosom'd deep in vines,
Where slumber abbots, purple as their wines:
To Isles of fragrance, lily-silver'd vales,
Diffusing languor in the panting gales:
To lands of singing, or of dancing slaves,
Love-whisp'ring woods, and lute-resounding waves . . .
Led by my hand, he saunter'd Europe round,
And gathered ev'ry Vice on Christian ground. . . .

Pope's final version of *The Dunciad* appeared in 1743. Two years earlier Lady Mary Wortley Montagu, who had inspired Pope with a violent passion that afterward degenerated into savage hatred, had visited Rome for the first time. By then a somewhat tarnished beauty, she was still, on occasion, "one of the most extraordinary shining characters in the world." At the moment, however, Lady Mary was herself suffering from the pangs of unrequited love, having become wildly infatuated with a young Italian homosexual named Francesco Algarotti. She was content to go to bed at ten and spend the morning hours running about "among the antiquities" and walking "every evening in a different beautiful villa," where, she wrote, she would have been completely happy "if amongst the fountains I could find the waters of Lethe," which would have washed away her griefs.

Although she does not describe it, the woman who, during her stay at Constantinople, had already penetrated the mosque of Santa Sophia in disguise would certainly have explored the Colosseum. Lady Mary loved antiquities, but she felt the coldest contempt for the great majority of her fellow tourists. They had earned themselves, she said, "the glorious title of Golden Asses all over Italy" because of their eagerness to squander English guineas on damaged pictures and clumsily repaired statues. At their worst these Golden Asses were equally acquisitive and ignorant, and contemptuous Italians, we are told, would often remark that "if the Colosseum were portable, the English would carry it away."

The Italians, however, are a common-sense people, and they soon grasped the practical advantages of the modern tourist trade. The fact that foreign travelers admired the Colosseum may have given it a new value. At any rate, in 1744 Pope Benedict XIV decided to

protect the ruins. He forbade the removal of stone from the fabric and consecrated the arena to the memory of the great multitude of Christian martyrs then thought to have perished there. In the center of the arena he planted a cross with the Stations of the Cross appropriately grouped around it. Benedict also ordered the erection of a pulpit, and there, every Friday, a poor Capuchin monk used to deliver a long untutored sermon.

This mixture of Christian and pagan images was particularly pleasing to the romantic English traveler. It gratified both his feeling for history and his new-found interest in the picturesque. Eighteenth-century Rome was full of similarly exciting contrasts. Nor was it to change much until the *risorgimento* and the birth of modern Italy. The Rome that Shelley knew in the second decade of the nineteenth century was still the city of the Georgian Grand Tourists. The population, Shelley wrote to his friend Peacock, was thinly scattered over a space "nearly as great as London. Wide wild fields are enclosed within it, and there are grassy lanes and copses winding among the ruins, and a great green hill, lonely and bare, which overhangs the Tiber. The gardens of the modern palaces are like wild woods of cedar, and cypress, and pine, and the neglected walks are overgrown with weeds."

An eighteenth-century traveler would also have recognized Shelley's picture of the Roman Forum — "a plain in the midst of Rome, a kind of desert full of stones and pits; and though so near the habitation of men . . . the most desolate place you can conceive. The ruins of temples stand in and around it, shattered columns and ranges of others complete, supporting

cornices of exquisite workmanship, and vast vaults of shattered domes distinct with regular compartments, once filled with sculptures of ivory or brass."

During the sixteenth and seventeenth centuries, however, there had still been some doubt as to the exact location of the ancient Forum, but many scholars agreed that it must lie beneath what was then called the Campo Vaccino, or cow pasture. In the sixth century the Ostrogoth leader Totila had declared that he would reduce the whole city to a place for grazing cattle, and although the barbarian's threat had not been executed, Nature and Time had had precisely the same effect upon what had been the civic heart of ancient Rome. Accumulated rubbish and the ruins of centuries had gradually blocked the Sacred Way and had buried the Forum itself and the spaces surrounding it under a tremendous load of earth and rubble.

An engraving by Giuseppe Vasi, executed in 1765, shows the aspect of the Campo Vaccino about the time of Edward Gibbon's first visit. An irregular avenue of trees runs down its length toward the distant Colosseum. On either side of the avenue stretch rough expanses of grass where peasant drovers watch their herds. Colonnades and triumphal arches stand half-buried in the Roman soil. As for the Colosseum, despite the cross erected by Pope Benedict XIV, parts of the arena had by then been let out for use as cowsheds and stables.

Toward the end of March 1765, James Boswell was exploring Rome and, at the same time, following his rakish fancy (sanctified, he liked to think, by the "behavior of Horace and other amorous Roman poets") among mercenary local girls. After a glimpse of "the

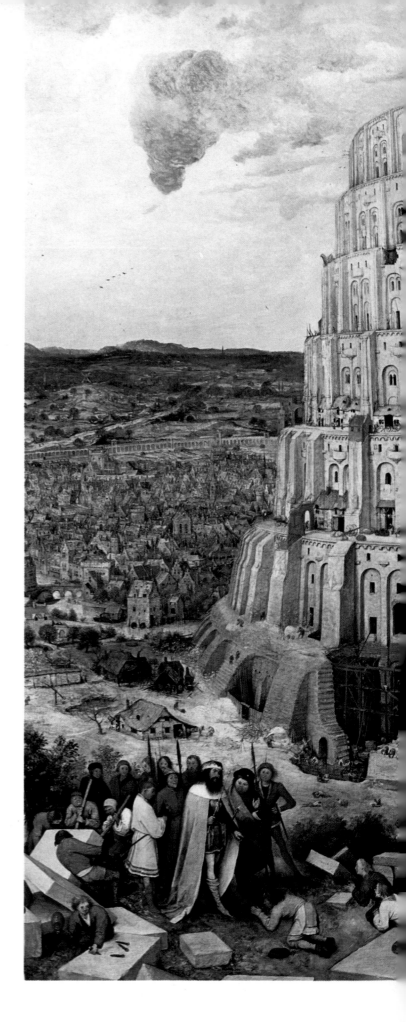

Romantic artists saw grandeur and beauty in the classic façade of the Colosseum, but Flemish artist Pieter Bruegel the Elder's vision was vastly different — his 1563 painting Building the Tower of Babel *transforms the arena into a monstrous yet fascinating caricature. To illustrate the Biblical tale of man's vanity and pretensions, Bruegel depicts the enormous edifice defiantly piercing the clouds while antlike workmen swarm about its lower levels.*

celebrated Forum," where, he noted, "the wretched huts of carpenters and other artisans" covered "the site of that rostrum from which Cicero had flung forth his stunning eloquence," he "entered the famous Colosseum, which certainly presents a vast and sublime idea of the grandeur of the ancient Romans. . . . A hermit has a little apartment inside. We passed through his hermitage to climb to where the seats and corridors once were. . . . It was shocking to discover several portions of this theatre full of dung."

Meanwhile the desolate grandeur of the Colosseum was beginning to interest English poets. Milton may have remembered the amphitheater when, in *Paradise Lost,* he told how the fallen angels built themselves a majestic meeting place, which they entitled *Pandae-monium,* where Satan held his solemn conclave:

Anon out of the earth a Fabrick huge
Rose like an Exhalation, with the sound
Of Dulcet Symphonies and voices sweet,
Built like a Temple, where *Pilasters* round
Were set, and Doric pillars overlaid
With Golden Architrave; nor did there want
Cornice or Freeze, with bossy Sculptures grav'n. . . .

The first English poet to describe the building at length, with any pretense of historical accuracy, was the amiable versifier John Dyer, whose literary survey *The Ruins of Rome* appeared in 1740. Dyer had been an itinerant artist before he settled down as a placid country clergyman, and his meditation on the wreck of the Colosseum has a peculiarly picturesque coloring:

Amid the towery ruins, huge, supreme,
The enormous amphitheatre behold,
Mountainous pile! o'er whose capacious womb

Pours the broad firmament its varied light,
While from the central floor the seats ascend
Round above round, slow-widening to the verge,
A circuit vast and high; nor less had held
Imperial Rome and her attendant realms,
When, drunk with rule, she will'd the fierce delight,
And op'd the gloomy caverns, whence out rush'd,
Before th' innumerable shouting crowd,
The fiery maddened tyrants of the wilds,
Lions and tigers, wolves and elephants,
And desperate men, more fell. Abhorr'd intent!
By frequent converse with familiar death
To kindle brutal daring apt for war;
To lock the breast, and steel th' obdurate heart,
Amid the piercing cries of sore distress
Impenetrable. — But away thine eye!

The emotions with which Rome itself inspired Dyer nevertheless were gently pensive and reflective:

How musical! when all-devouring Time,
Here sitting on his throne of ruins hoar,
While winds and tempests sweep his various lyre,
How sweet thy diapason, Melancholy!

There was nothing melancholy, however, about the mood of Edward Gibbon when his carriage rattled across the Milvian Bridge in October 1764. The next morning he entered the Campo Vaccino and looked around him at all that remained of the Palatine and Capitol. "Several days of intoxication" followed, before he recollected that he was a serious student of the past rather than a romantic dilettante and he could settle down to "a cool and minute investigation" of the most important Roman ruins. The guide he chose was James Byers, a Scotsman long established in Rome,

who combined the roles of banker, travel agent, and professional archaeologist. The series of tours that Byers organized were to occupy Gibbon for more than four months.

It was early in his visit that Gibbon conceived his master plan. The moment of illumination that kindled his genius occurred on October 15. As darkness fell, he sat near the threshold of a gaunt medieval church, Santa Maria in Aracoeli, which he believed — though, in fact, he was misinformed — to have replaced the golden-roofed Temple of Jupiter on the Capitoline. There, hearing the evening hymn, sung by barefooted Franciscan monks, rolling through the church's open doors, he suddenly recognized his true vocation. It was then, we learn from Gibbon's autobiography, that "the idea of writing the decline and fall of the city first started to my mind." He would not complete *The Decline and Fall of the Roman Empire* until July 27, 1787, twenty-two years later; the last volumes of this tremendous undertaking appeared in April 1788. Gibbon kept back his only detailed account of the Colosseum for his final pages, but the amphitheater had undoubtedly helped to determine his attitude toward the Roman people — an attitude of deep, involuntary respect, often mixed with fear and horror.

Less than a year before Edward Gibbon reluctantly laid aside his manuscript, another man of genius entered Rome. Johann Wolfgang von Goethe, a superbly handsome young man of thirty-three, passed beneath the Porta del Popolo on November 1, 1786, and only then did he feel entirely confident that he would reach his destination — he had so long looked forward to seeing Rome and so many anxious thoughts

had assailed him as he traveled south.

An "irresistible impulse" had drawn Goethe to Italy. During his childhood he had been profoundly excited by the prints of Roman antiquities that his father, a Frankfurt lawyer, had brought home from an Italian visit. And later the impulse had become "a kind of disease," which he discovered he could not expect to cure except "by the sight and presence of the absent object."

Accompanying him was the artist Johann Tischbein, who was afterward to paint his friend's portrait, in white cloak and broad-brimmed hat, brooding among the ruined tombs of the Campagna. But soon after their arrival Tischbein portrayed his friend gazing down into a busy street from the window of their Roman inn. Goethe's back is turned toward the artist, and Max Beerbohm, in one of his later essays, has described the impression that the drawing makes:

> It is a graceful, a forceful and a noble back. . . . Had Napoleon been there to see it, he would have murmured, as . . . he did when he saw Goethe face to face at Weimar in later years, *Voila un homme!* It is moreover the back of a man wrapped in contemplation . . . a man avidly observing, learning, storing up. He is wearing slippers, he has not yet put on his waistcoat nor buttoned his breeches at the knee. His toilet can wait. His passionate curiosity cannot. It is as intimate, as significant a portrait as ever was made of one man by another.

Goethe's curiosity, with its extraordinary keenness and range, was always a distinguishing feature of his intellectual constitution. Nothing escaped him; no problem was too small or too large to engage that puissant mind — from the most effective method of avoiding seasickness to Italian recipes for manufacturing *pasta*, from botany and minor points of zoology to the idea he was patiently working out that every species had its source in some primeval basic form in which were already comprised all its possibilities of development. Goethe was both a poet and a scientist, a man who loved flowers as much as he liked fossils. At Venice he had already spent happy days investigating "the structure of cuttlefish and the habits of crabs," which he dredged out of the waters of the lagoon. And when he continued his journey to Sicily, he watched a school of dolphins, which leaped and played beside the vessel, noting how, as they sprang into the air, the light that shimmered along their glistening bodies changed from gold to green, and then from green to gold.

Rome occupied Goethe's attention for four months, and although he left the city on February 21, 1787, he returned to follow up his studies at the beginning of June. The first reference to the Colosseum in his journal was made on November 11, 1786, ten days after he arrived in the city. That morning he had journeyed down the Appian Way and admired the "solid masonry" of the tomb of Cecilia Metella, which he found even more interesting than the tomb's romantic legend. Finally he reached the great amphitheater:

> In the evening we came upon the Colosseum, when it was already twilight. When one looks at it all else seems little; the edifice is so vast, that one cannot hold the image of it in one's soul — in memory we think it smaller, and then return to it again to find it every time greater than before.

His second description of the Colosseum, on February 2, 1787, is an especially characteristic piece of writing. The moon had risen over Rome, and the sky was unclouded:

> For three several days we have enjoyed . . . the brightest and most glorious of nights. Peculiarly beautiful at such a time is the Colosseum. At night it is always closed; a hermit dwells in a little shrine within its range, and beggars of all kinds nestle beneath its crumbling arches. The latter had lit a fire on the arena, and a gentle wind bore down the smoke to the ground, so that the lower portion of the ruins was quite hid by it, while above the vast walls stood out in deeper darkness. . . . As we stopped at the gate to contemplate the scene through the iron gratings, the moon shone brightly in the heavens above. Presently the smoke found its way up the sides, and through every chink and opening, while the moon lit it up like a cloud.

Typical of Goethe is the sharp poetic eye that picks out not only the gigantic masses of the darkened amphitheater but the strange and elusive effect produced by clouds of drifting smoke. After his momentous visit to Rome, he was never quite the same man. Like Gibbon he had discovered his true vocation and he had established a standard of judgment that was to govern all his future writing. At the same time, he had detected "two of my capital faults," which had hampered him throughout his whole career:

> One is that in any business I wanted, or ought, to undertake, I would never learn the *workmanship*. Therefore it is that with so much natural talent I have done and accomplished so little. All my accomplishments have been extorted . . . by sheer force of mind. . . . The other fault . . . is that I would never devote so much time to any work or business as was required. . . . A regular progressive execution was irksome and at last intolerable to me.

The influence of Rome on Goethe's spirit was at once exciting and relaxing. There he revived two unfinished works, *Egmont* and *Iphigenie auf Tauris*, and added fresh scenes to the tragedy of *Faust*. Meanwhile, all his bodily senses — notably those of sight and touch — seemed to have acquired a new acuteness, "and through greater awareness of the particular [he] was the better able to apprehend the universal." Rome had taught him how to live, and on his return to the petty state of Weimar, where since 1775 he had served as an industrious court official, he took with him, besides his verse dramas, the plan of his romantic and erotic *Roman Elegies*. To Gibbon, Rome had revealed the past; to Goethe, a vision of human life that comprehended past and present. Henceforward, thanks to the lessons he had learned, he hoped to realize his genius and live in "peace and joy."

VII

WHILE STANDS THE COLOSSEUM

The world in which Gibbon and Goethe had flourished — the old world of hereditary power and privilege — was very soon to disappear. During the year that followed Goethe's return from Rome, news of the French Revolution astonished Europe. Like the French *philosophes*, Gibbon was bewildered by an event for which his own writings had effectively prepared the way. He regarded the Revolution as an attack of "popular madness," and he was deeply concerned about the fate of old friends whom the upheaval scattered far and wide. Life at Rome, too, lost its patrician dignity. Although the French Ambassador, Casanova's one-time friend the Cardinal de Bernis — who had long kept open house at the Palazzo de Carolis — gallantly stuck to his post until his death in 1794, most of the distinguished foreigners he had entertained immediately called for their carriages and hurried homeward.

Finally, Napoleon attacked the Papal States. In 1798 Pope Pius VI, who had already denounced the Civil Constitution of the Clergy, was removed to the French prison at Valence, where he spent his last days. His successor, Pius VII, received even more outrageous treatment. Despite the concordat he had signed with Napoleon — and the diplomatic attitude he adopted in 1804 when he agreed to attend the emperor's coronation at Notre-Dame de Paris and sat by watching as Napoleon placed the crown upon his own head — Pius in 1809 was deprived of his temporal authority, and the whole extent of the Papal States was summarily annexed to France.

The pope's protests and the bulls of excommunication he issued were met by the emperor with a show of armed might, although Napoleon later denied that he had given definite orders for the pope to be arrested. But in June 1809, the Roman bridges were blocked, a Neapolitan regiment with bandsmen marching at its head took possession of the city, and from the Castel Sant'Angelo was displayed for the first time not the ancient papal standard, but the tricolor ensign of the Napoleonic Empire. Subsequently, one of Napoleon's most zealous subordinates, having employed a hatchet to break the locks, burst into the pope's room. Pius was then hurried away to a coach and carried off to French captivity. At Fontainebleau the pope had expected to meet his captor, but Napoleon was by then en route to Moscow. Pius remained a captive at Fontainebleau while the emperor was elsewhere, fighting his last victorious battles.

French occupation did not permanently change Rome, but it had at least a passing effect upon the Flavian Amphitheater. The French troops, like troops of every nation, showed little interest in antiquities. The Basilica of Constantine, which they used as a drill ground and riding school, lost almost all of the interior decorations that had thus far survived. But Napoleon brought his archaeologists with him to Rome as he had brought them to Egypt in 1798. And though modern Rome pleased the disorderly English, with their romantic taste for ruins, it often offended French scholars, with their inherited love of style and symmetry. Late in the eighteenth century, the erudite Charles de Brosses suggested — when he described his promenades around Rome — that the Colosseum, already so sadly decayed, should be cut in half by demolishing all the most seriously damaged portions to reduce the amphitheater to a demiamphitheater, which might overlook an impressive fountain or, perhaps, an artificial lake. Napoleon's experts were slightly less ruthless, but they considered that the Colosseum needed careful tidying up. Plants and shrubs had overgrown its fabric, and in 1812 they advised that the ruins should be methodically stripped and weeded.

With Napoleon's fall, Rome reverted to its former antique quietude. But although the emperor had vanished, the spirit he had raised — a spirit of adventure and unrest — lingered on in the Romantic movement. After Waterloo a horde of tourists returned, and among them came some of the young Romantic poets who were creating a new heaven and a new earth. Keats, Shelley, and Byron all visited Rome at important moments in their lives.

Keats, alas, was far too ill and weary to enjoy his strange surroundings. He and his friend the artist Joseph Severn passed the Colosseum on the way to the rooms they had hired in the Piazza di Spagna. But until his illness reached its crucial stage and he at last abandoned hope, if Keats left his lodgings at all it was usually to ride around the gardens on the nearby Pincian Hill, where he often caught some disturbing glimpses of Princess Pauline Borghese, Napoleon's lovely, ill-conducted sister.

Shelley was more fortunate. In Rome he discovered the proper background of some of his wildest poetic fancies. For the "mountainous ruins of the Baths of Caracalla" he developed an especial liking. It was there, "among the flowery glades and thickets of odoriferous blossoming trees, which are extended in ever widening labyrinths upon its immense platforms and dizzy arches," that the poet worked on the manuscript of

Prometheus Unbound. And it was there that Severn painted his portrait — a large-eyed waif, musing in solitude above the pages of an open book.

Shelley was also deeply impressed by the Flavian Amphitheater:

The Coliseum [he wrote to Thomas Love Peacock in 1818] is unlike any work of human hands I ever saw before. It is of enormous height and circuit, and the arches built of massive stones are piled on one another, and jut into the blue air, shattered into the forms of overhanging rocks. It has been changed by time into an amphitheatre of rocky hills overgrown by the wild olive, the myrtle, and the fig tree, and threaded by little paths, which wind among its ruined stairs and immeasurable galleries: the copsewood overshadows you as you wander through its labyrinths, and the wild weeds of this climate of flowers bloom under your feet. The arena is covered with grass, and pierces, like the skirts of a natural plain, the chasms of the broken arches around. But a small part of the exterior circumference remains — it is exquisitely light and beautiful . . . the interior is all ruin. I can scarcely believe that when encrusted with Dorian marble and ornamented by columns of Egyptian granite, its effect could have been so sublime and so impressive . . . it is open to the sky, and it was the clear and sunny weather of the end of November . . . when we visited it, day after day. . . .

Shelley flitted around Rome with his customary wraith-like stealth and speed. His friend, Byron, however, drove into the Eternal City on April 29, 1817, in his usual worldly, dashing manner — accompanied by a retinue of servants, three or four saddle horses, and Mütz, a shaggy Swiss mastiff, one of the huge devoted dogs that always followed his emblazoned carriage. He came from Venice, where for the last few months he had been leading an enjoyable carefree life. But the amusements of the Venetian Carnival and the exactions of a new mistress both made him feel that he deserved a holiday; and since his old friend John Cam Hobhouse was then in Rome, he had chosen to undertake a southern tour.

Byron was no dilettante. Painting he detested, "unless it reminds me of something I have seen or think it possible to see. . . ." Nor was he deeply interested in any of the other arts. Yet when he passed through Florence, he found time to admire not only the Venus de'Medici but also pictures by Raphael, Titian, and Michelangelo. And when he reached Rome, he declared that, "as a *whole, ancient* and *modern,* it beats Greece, Constantinople, every thing — at least that I have ever seen." He could not describe the city, he added, so "strong and confused" were his immediate sensations.

Meanwhile, besides jogging about Rome and collecting the rich poetic materials that his memory was to select and arrange in a further canto of *Childe Harold,* he viewed "the pope alive, and a cardinal dead — both of whom looked very well indeed," and he even plucked up courage to attend a public execution. "The ceremony — including the *masqued* priests; the half-naked executioners; the bandaged criminals; the black Christ and his banner . . . the quick rattle and fall of the axe; the splash of the blood" — struck him as "altogether more impressive" than its vulgar English counterpart, though the first death "turned me quite hot and thirsty, and made me shake so that I could hardly hold the opera-glass. . . ."

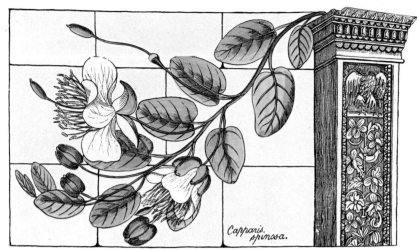

Otherwise until he had returned to Venice, Byron merely announced that Rome was "indescribable" and that its monuments were "inconceivable." At Venice he started work on Canto IV of his famous poem, and a new Childe Harold emerged, bringing the work to a splendid climax. Byron, of course, could never escape from himself or from the recollection of his own sorrows, but during the three weeks that he had spent exploring Rome, his tragic vision of human existence acquired a novel depth and sharpness. Like Saint Jerome, he laments the plight of the city that had once "taken captive all the world":

> The Niobe of nations! there she stands,
> Childless and crownless, in her voiceless woe;
> An empty urn within her withered hands,
> Whose holy dust was scattered long ago. . . .

> The Goth, the Christian — Time — War — Flood, and
>   Fire,
> Have dealt upon the seven-hilled City's pride;
> She saw her glories star by star expire,
> And up the steep barbarian Monarchs ride,
> Where the car climbed the Capitol; far and wide
> Temple and tower went down, nor left a site: —
> Chaos of ruins! who shall trace the void,
> O'er the dim fragments cast a lunar light,
> And say, "here was, or is, where all is doubly night!"

In *Childe Harold,* as in many of his other works, Byron, a gifted rhetorician, is often content to strike the appropriate romantic pose. But in his pictures of the tomb of Cecilia Metella, the ruined Palatine, and the Colosseum, despite some discordant rhetorical touches, he displays a much more moving eloquence

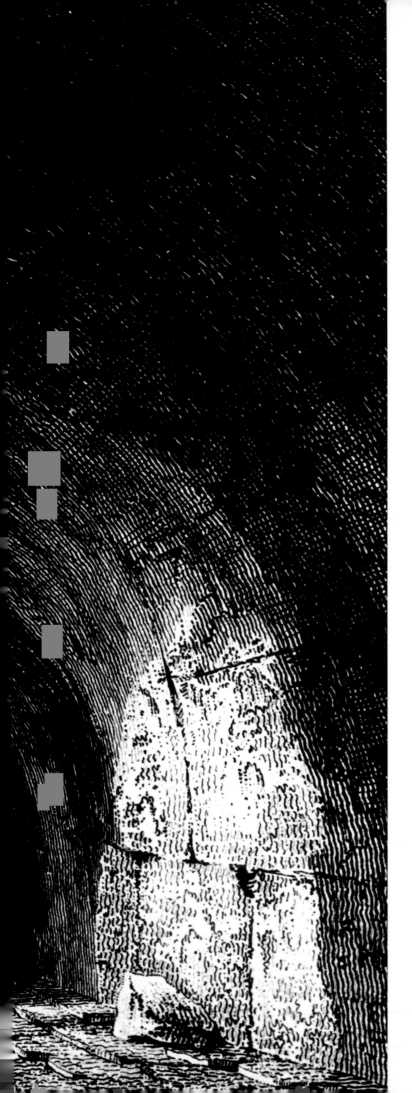

By the time Lord Byron visited the Colosseum, a verdant tangle of wildflowers, low shrubs, and strangling vines had overgrown the entire ruin. This 1841 engraving shows the "garland-forest" that the poet described in his epic work Childe Harold.

and achieves an imaginative synthesis between the present and the past — between his own emotions and the symbol he contemplates — that lifts rhetoric toward the heaven of poetry.

His description of the Colosseum alone occupies eleven stanzas. They are of unequal value; and his vivid glimpse of the dying gladiator (probably inspired by the statue of a dying Gaul that he admired in the museum of the Capitol) is far too celebrated to need quotation. But no account of the Flavian Amphitheater, and of its effect on the men and women who have visited it, would be complete without the closing passages:

> But here, where Murder breathed her bloody steam: —
> And here, where buzzing nations choked the ways,
> And roared or murmured like a mountain stream
> Dashing or winding as its torrent strays;
> Here, where the Roman million's blame or praise
> Was Death or Life — the plaything of a crowd —
> My voice sounds much — and fall the stars' faint rays
> On the arena void — seats crushed — walls bowed —
> And galleries, where my steps seem echoes strangely
>   loud. . . .
> But when the rising moon begins to climb
> Its topmost arch, and gently pauses there —
> When the stars twinkle through the loops of Time,
> And the low night-breeze waves along the air
> The garland-forest, which the gray walls wear,
> Like laurels on the bald first Caesar's head —
> When the light shines serene but doth not glare —
> Then in this magic circle raise the dead;
> Heroes have trod this spot — 'tis on their dust ye tread.

While he remained at Rome, Byron must often have stood within the moonlit Colosseum; on one occasion

123

his purpose was not to raise the dead but to call down vengeance on the living. He had arrived in Italy bearing the heavy burden of guilt that he owed to his illicit passion for his half-sister and haunted by what he had earlier called "the nightmare of my own delinquencies." Nevertheless, he harbored bitter grudges, which concerned both his "unforgiving" wife and her parents and advisers, and he managed to persuade himself that he had been vilely traduced and deeply injured.

One of his chief legal assassins he believed to have been Sir Samuel Romilly, a high-minded London advocate and distinguished Whig reformer. Early in November 1818, after losing the wife he adored, Romilly committed suicide. The news caused Byron horrid glee. He then seized the opportunity of addressing Lady Byron in a singularly unattractive letter. "Sir Samuel Romilly," he remarked, "has cut his throat for the loss of his wife. It is now nearly three years since he became . . . the Approver of the proceedings, which deprived me of mine." Little, he went on, could Romilly have then supposed that "in less than thirty-six moons . . . a domestic affliction would lay him in the earth, with the meanest of malefactors. . . . It was not in vain that I invoked Nemesis in the midnight of Rome from the awfullest of her ruins." To his publisher, John Murray, he threw out a similarly alarming hint: "So Sir Samuel Romilly has cut his throat. . . . You see that Nemesis is not yet extinct, for I had not forgot Sir S. in my imprecation, which involved many." Perhaps Lady Byron may have been among those on whom the poet called down curses.

During his years of fame and fortune, Byron had few rivals. But there was one fellow man of genius who seems to have occasioned the poet uneasy feelings, and it has been suggested that, if Byron never visited France, it was because he wished to keep a decent distance between himself and the famous author of *René*. Byron and Chateaubriand evidently had much in common: each was proud of his aristocratic birth; each had a devoted sister who loved him far too well; each, after a difficult childhood, philandered passionately and traveled widely; and each cultivated a form of romantic egotism from which he drew his literary strength. Finally, each appears to have possessed the knack of arranging his personal career in a dramatic and symbolic pattern. Byron, who had spent the happiest period of his youth traveling among the Greek islands, returned to end his life on Greek soil. Chateaubriand had two contrasted views both of England — first as a penniless outcast, then as an affluent ambassador — and of the Eternal City. Having seen Rome in 1803 as an unimportant secretary, he revisited the city in 1828 as the honored representative of King Charles X.

Like Byron, Chateaubriand opened his heart to Rome. He was never tired, he said on his second visit, of wandering across the Campagna or botanizing near the tomb of Cecilia Metella, where "the ripple of mignonette and the blue windflowers of the Apennines" harmonized with the whiteness of the walls. He wished that he himself might have a Roman tomb; Rome, he felt, was the perfect place "in which to forget all, to despise all and to die." Even on his first visit, though only thirty-five, Chateaubriand had often thought of death, for his chief companion at that time had been a dying woman.

Pauline de Beaumont, one of the most delicate and

sympathetic of Chateaubriand's many mistresses, had decided to join him in the city. She was not beautiful — her face was pinched and thin — and the fire in her almond-shaped eyes, he wrote, might perhaps have seemed unduly brilliant had they not been tempered by an air of languishing gentlenesss, as a ray of sunlight is subdued when it passes through a glass of water. Her present pathetic condition brought out in Chateaubriand everything that was the noblest, kindliest, and least self-centered. He nursed her tenderly at the little house, close to the Piazza di Spagna, where she spent her last weeks. Toward the end of October, when death was fast approaching, he took her to the Colosseum. It was a delightfully warm day:

> She succeeded in leaving the carriage and sat down upon a stone facing one of the altars . . . she lifted her eyes; she allowed them to wander slowly over these portals, dead themselves so many years, that in their time had seen so many deaths; the ruins were decked with briars and columbines which the autumn had tinged saffron-yellow . . . the dying woman allowed her farewell gaze to descend from step to step; it came to rest on the cross of the altar, and she said to me: "Let us go; I am cold." I accompanied her back to her room; she went to bed and never rose again.

During that same visit, after Pauline de Beaumont's death, Chateaubriand gave a much more ambitious account of the ruins of the Colosseum in his memorable letter to Fontanes. Now he sat alone on the steps of one of the Christian altars raised there:

> The setting sun poured floods of golden light through all those galleries down which had once rolled the torrent of the Roman peoples; at the same time, heavy shadows fell from the deep embrasures of the boxes and the passages, or drew large black stripes across the earth. From the summit of the craggy heaps of masonry, between the ruins of the building's right side, I saw the gardens of the Palatine. . . . Instead of the roars of joy uttered by ferocious spectators as they watched Christians torn apart by lions, one heard only the barking of the hermit's dogs. . . . But, as soon as the sun had vanished, the bell on the dome of St. Peter's reverberated beneath the Colosseum's arches.

No English version can hope to do justice to the solemn undulatory music of the master's prose style; and compared with Chateaubriand, neither Germaine de Staël nor Marie Henri Beyle — though both of them were deeply attached to Rome — proves a very good reporter. Since the publication of her *Letters on the Works and Character of Jean-Jacques Rousseau* in 1788, Madame de Staël had been a Parisian celebrity and a powerful literary hostess. No one appreciated success more. When she was two months old, her mother, wife of the great financier Jacques Necker, reported that little Germaine was already "very impatient to begin talking"; and once she had fully mastered the art, her flow of conversation seldom flagged. As she swept up and down Europe, this stout, tempestuous lady gave her views on every current question, and her ideas and prejudices, which were sometimes highly unorthodox, overflowed into the books she wrote.

Madame de Staël's novel *Corinne*, inspired by a visit to Italy, appeared in the year 1807. Its heroine is a romanticized self-portrait; its hero, a consumptive Scottish nobleman. But although Corinne and Oswald, Lord Nevil, presently look into the Colosseum, their visit to this "superb edifice, the most beautiful ruin of Rome," merely provides an excuse for eloquent moralizing on the theme of human liberty and on the value we should attach to "natural sentiments." Elsewhere Madame de Staël makes fun of the poor Capuchin who delivered the traditional Friday sermon, remarking that it was difficult to respect a preacher whose knowledge of the history of the world was limited to his own existence. She was interested, however, to observe a fraternity of Roman penitents — dressed in large gray hoods that entirely concealed their faces — at their prayers among the ruins, and watch them fall to their knees loudly imploring the divine mercy.

Marie Henri Beyle, better known as Stendhal, who perambulated Rome in 1828, two years before his novel *Le Rouge et le Noir* appeared, was considerably less sententious than Madame de Staël. He enjoyed admiring the stately background of art, though his real preoccupation was with men and manners, and the curious behavior of ignorant English tourists was always a rewarding subject:

Some days ago [he writes in his *Promenades dans Rome*] an Englishman arrived . . . with his horses which had brought him from his native land. He did not wish for a guide, and, despite the efforts of the sentinel, rode straight into the Colosseum. There he saw some hundred masons and galley-slaves working to consolidate a piece of wall that had been weakened by the rain. . . . "By God," he said to us that evening, "the Colosseum is the best thing I have seen in Rome. It will be a magnificent building when it's finished."

Stendhal's reference to the hundred masons and prisoners at work upon the Colosseum reminds us that,

since the beginning of the nineteenth century, the papal government had taken an active interest in the restoration of Rome's most famous ruin. First, Pius VII had strengthened the east end. Then, in 1825, Leo XII had supported its western circumference with the erection of a massive buttress. Turner's sketch, made in 1819, depicts the southwestern façade with a ragged broken edge. Corot's enchanting view of the amphitheater from the gardens on the Palatine shows it after restoration. Later, in 1845 and 1852, Gregory XVI and Pius IX continued to repair the arena, which gradually lost the air of romantic decrepitude that had so fascinated eighteenth-century travelers.

The Colosseum, however, had not yet been stripped of its luxuriant flowers and foliage, for once the French had retired from the city in 1812, the vegetation had soon come back. For some tourists, the flora of the Colosseum was its greatest beauty. Of all the wondrous things he had seen, wrote the American landscape painter Thomas Cole in 1832, the Colosseum was the object that had most affected him:

From the broad arena within, it rises around, arch above arch, broken and desolate, and mantled in many parts with the laurustinus, the acanthus, and numerous other plants and flowers. . . . It looks more like a work of nature than of man. . . . The regularity of art is lost . . . in dilapidation. . . . Crag rises over crag; green and breezy summits mount into the sky.

Indeed, the vegetation that covered the Colosseum became a subject that engrossed botanists. As early as 1813, Antonio Sebastiani, author of *Flora Colisea*, listed 261 species that he had discovered growing there; in 1855, the Englishman Richard Deakin, when he pub-

lished his *Flora of the Colosseum,* added nearly 160 more. Many trees flourished on lofty ledges — the fig, the cherry, the pear, and the elm. The ruins also supported vines and ivy, clematis and wild roses; and the stonework was pied and dappled with an exquisite variety of small plants, which included rosemary, thyme, sage, cyclamen, daisies, pimpernels, hyacinths, saxifrage, violets, strawberries, marigolds, and larkspur. Some of the rarer species, enthusiasts claimed, were otherwise unknown in Europe. It was even suggested that their seeds had been brought to Rome among the foodstuffs provided for exotic animals destined to be killed during the *venationes.*

At last, in 1871, the Italian archaeologist Pietro Rosa was allowed to strip the ruins naked. Somewhat later the central cross was removed, as were the Stations of the Cross that had formerly encircled it. Rome by then was the capital of a united Italy, and in 1885 the hideous Victor Emmanuel monument — built to commemorate unification — began to emerge on the flank of the Capitoline.

Meanwhile Rome had continued to slumber and decay, and only once were its slumbers disturbed by the upheavals of nineteenth-century Europe. The backwash of the Year of Revolutions, 1848, affected even Rome itself. In November the pope's minister, Count Pellegrino Rossi, was assassinated on the threshold of the Palazzo della Cancellaria, and Pope Pius IX fled to the conservative Kingdom of Naples, whence he thundered against malevolent foreign demagogues and demanded the submission of his ungrateful city.

Early the next year, a Roman Republic was proclaimed, with Giuseppe Mazzini as one of its triumvirs and Giuseppe Garibaldi as its military guardian. Both were patriots of the most exalted type. "Rome was to me . . ." declared Mazzini, "in spite of her present degradation . . . the Temple of Humanity." Passing beneath the Porta del Popolo, he added, "I felt an electric thrill run through me — a spring of new life." No less romantic was the mood of Garibaldi and his followers:

> The sculptor Gibson [writes a contemporary diarist] . . . describes the spectacle offered by these wild-looking warriors . . . as one of the strangest ever witnessed in the Eternal City. The men sunburnt, with long unkempt hair, wearing conical-shaped hats with black waving plumes; their gaunt, dust-soiled faces framed with shaggy beards . . . crowding round their chief, who rode a white horse, perfectly statuesque in virile beauty; the whole group looking more like a company of brigands out of some picture of Salvator Rosa than a disciplined military force.

Soon after he had entered the city, however, Mazzini admitted to the English poet Arthur Clough that his hopes were slowly sinking. France, Austria, Spain, and Naples had all rallied to the pope's support. Rome was besieged, and despite a gallant defense, a French army managed to breach the ramparts. Amid savage hand-to-hand fighting, Garibaldi led a last charge. At the end of June, the Roman Republic collapsed, and in 1850, Pius IX, once a well-meaning liberal pontiff, now a hardened reactionary, was reinstated as a temporal sovereign. That position he retained until September 1870, when — Napoleon III having withdrawn his troops at the outbreak of the Franco-Prussian War — a column of Bersagliere (a corps of sharpshooters)

marched into Rome. The Middle Ages, wrote the historian Ferdinand Gregorovius, were finally blown away as by a strong north wind. Pius IX became a self-appointed prisoner of the Vatican; Rome, the thriving center of a prosperous modern kingdom.

It is difficult not to regret the old Rome, which, before the *risorgimento,* must have been one of the most beautiful cities on earth — a shabby, sleepy place, where the pope still rode abroad, blessing the crowd from his resplendent palanquin; purple judas trees leaned over garden walls; baroque fountains splashed in quiet squares; and everywhere hulks of ancient stonework, defaced friezes, and weathered Corinthian columns rubbed shoulders with Renaissance masonry. This was the Rome that delighted Henry Wadsworth Longfellow but offended Charles Dickens. Longfellow had visited Rome for the first time as early as 1828, and like other poetic visitors, he hastened to record his impressions of the Colosseum. Naturally, he inspected the arena by moonlight:

> At length I came to an open space where the arches above had crumbled away, leaving the pavement an unroofed terrace high in air. From this point, I could see the whole interior of the amphitheatre spread out beneath me, half in shadow, half in light, with such soft and indefinite outline that it seemed less an earthly reality than a reflection in the bosom of a lake. . . .

Longfellow's last visit, when he was painted by the American artist George Peter Alexander Healy — wearing overcoat and top hat, promenading beneath the Arch of Titus, with his youthful daughter on his arm — took place in 1869. The Colosseum had not yet lost its flowers, and Longfellow wrote of them in the verse-

drama *Michael Angelo* that he did not live to finish:

> A thousand wild flowers bloom
> From every chink, and the birds build their nests
> Among the ruined arches . . .

Dickens arrived in 1846, and his immediate impressions of Rome were peculiarly disappointing. January 30, he reports, was "a dark muddy day. . . ."

> We had crossed the Tiber by the Ponte Molle. . . . It had looked as yellow as it ought to look, and hurrying on between its worn away and miry banks, had a promising aspect of desolation and ruin. . . . [But] There were no great ruins, no solemn tokens of antiquity to be seen. . . . There seemed to be long streets of commonplace shops and houses, such as are to be found in any European town. . . . It was no more my Rome . . . than the Place de la Concorde in Paris is.

Nor was he pleased with the modern Romans, whose faces, he wrote in *Pictures from Italy,* were not ill-suited to the ancient function of the Colosseum:

> As it tops the other ruins: standing there, a mountain among graves: so do its ancient influences outlive all other remnants of the old mythology and old butchery of Rome, in the nature of the fierce and cruel Roman people. The Italian face changes as the visitor approaches the city; its beauty becomes devilish; and there is scarcely one countenance in a hundred, among the common people in the streets, that would not be at home and happy in a renovated Coliseum tomorrow.
>
> Here was Rome indeed at last; and such a Rome as no one can imagine in its full and awful grandeur!

Dickens thanked God that the amphitheater was now a ruin. Yet being an artist as well as a moralist, he was not insensitive to its monumental beauty:

THE COLOSSEUM
IN LITERATURE

AN ARENA
FOR
IMPERIAL ROME

One of the Colosseum's earliest admirers, the Roman poet Martial, wrote the world's first book about the arena and its spectacles in A.D. 80, the year the amphitheater was opened to the public. The first verses of Martial's work intimate that the Colosseum surpassed in splendor the seven wonders of the ancient world: Egypt's pyramids, Babylon's hanging gardens, Ephesus' Temple of Diana, the mausoleum at Halicarnassus, the Colossus of Rhodes, the statue of Olympian Zeus in Greece, and the palace of Cyrus in Persia. Other verses celebrate the arena's construction and describe the first contests held there. Following are prose translations.

Let not barbaric Memphis tell of the wonder of her Pyramids, nor Assyrian toil vaunt its Babylon; let not the soft Ionians be extolled for Trivia's fane; let the altar wrought of many horns keep hid its Delos; let not Carians exalt to the skies with boundless praise the Mausoleum poised on empty air. All labour yields to Caesar's Amphitheatre: one work in place of all shall Fame rehearse.

Here where, rayed with stars, the Colossus [statue of Nero] views heaven anear, and in the middle way tall scaffolds rise, hatefully gleamed the palace of a savage king, and but a single house now stood in the City. Here, where the far-seen Amphitheatre lifts its mass august, was Nero's mere. Here, where we admire the warm-baths, a gift swiftly wrought, a proud domain had robbed their dwellings from the poor. Where the Claudian Colonnade extends its outspread shade the Palace ended in its farthest part. Rome has been restored to herself, and under thy governance, Caesar [Titus], that is now the delight of a people which was once a master's.

The crucifixion of the thief Laureolus and his subsequent mutilation by wild beasts was reenacted in the arena using a condemned prisoner who was himself crucified. Martial reported on the gory spectacle.

As, fettered on a Scythian crag, Prometheus fed the untiring fowl with his too prolific heart, so Laureolus, hanging on no unreal cross, gave up his vitals defenceless to a Caledonian bear. His mangled limbs lived, though the parts dripped gore, and in all his body was nowhere a body's shape. A punishment deserved at length he won — he in his guilt had with his sword pierced his parent's or his master's throat, or in his madness robbed a temple of its close-hidden gold, or had laid by stealth his savage torch to thee, O Rome. Accursed, he had outdone the crimes told of by ancient lore; in him that which had been a show before was punishment.

Martial singled out Carpophorus, a hunter of wild beasts, for special praise.

He plunged his hunter's spear also in a headlong-rushing bear, the king of beasts beneath the cope of Arctic skies; and he laid low a lion, magnificent, of bulk unknown before, one worthy of Hercules' might; and with a far-dealt wound stretched in death a rushing pard [leopard]. He won the prize of honour; yet unbroken still was his strength.

MARTIAL
Epigrams, A.D. 80

English historian Edward Gibbon's The Decline and Fall of the Roman
Empire *is unquestionably the best-known history of imperial Rome ever
written. The book made its author famous almost overnight, and it is still
regarded as a classic of its kind. Gibbon first visited Rome at the im-
pressionable age of twenty-five, and there he made the decision that would
ultimately bring him enduring fame: "It was in Rome, on the fifteenth of
October, 1764, as I sat musing amidst the ruins of the Capitol, while the
barefooted friars were singing vespers in the temple of Jupiter, that the
idea of writing the decline and fall of the city first started to my mind."
Many of the Colosseum's bloodiest spectacles — among them the excesses
of Emperor Commodus — were graphically recorded by Gibbon.*

Every sentiment of virtue and humanity was extinct in the mind of
Commodus. Whilst he thus abandoned the reins of empire to these unworthy favorites, he valued nothing in sovereign power, except the un-
bounded licence of indulging his sensual appetites. His hours were spent
in a seraglio of three hundred beautiful women, and as many boys, of every
rank, and of every province; and, wherever the arts of seduction proved
ineffectual, the brutal lover had recourse to violence. The ancient historians
have expatiated on these abandoned scenes of prostitution, which scorned
every restraint of nature or modesty; but it would not be easy to translate
their too faithful descriptions into the decency of modern language. The
intervals of lust were filled up with the basest amusements. The influence of
a polite age, and the labour of an attentive education, had never been able
to infuse into his brutish mind, the least tincture of learning; and he was
the first of the Roman emperors totally devoid of taste for the pleasures of
the understanding. Nero himself excelled, or affected to excel, in the elegant
arts of music and poetry; nor should we despise his pursuits, had he not
converted the pleasing relaxation of a leisure hour into the serious business
and ambition of his life. But Commodus, from his earliest infancy, discovered an aversion to whatever was rational or liberal, and a fond attachment to the amusements of the populace; the sports of the circus and amphitheatre, the combats of gladiators, and the hunting of wild beasts. The
masters in every branch of learning, whom Marcus [Commodus's father]
provided for his son, were heard with inattention and disgust; whilst the
Moors and Parthians, who taught him to dart the javelin and to shoot with
the bow, found a disciple who delighted in his application, and soon equalled
the most skilful of his instructors. . . .

The servile crowd, whose fortune depended on their master's vices,
applauded these ignoble pursuits. The perfidious voice of flattery reminded
him, that by exploits of the same nature, by the defeat of the Nemaean lion,
and the slaughter of the wild boar of Erymanthus, the Grecian Hercules had
acquired a place among the gods, and an immortal memory among men.
They only forgot to observe, that, in the first ages of society, when the fiercer
animals often dispute with man the possession of an unsettled country, a
successful war against those savages is one of the most innocent and bene-
ficial labours of heroism. In the civilized state of the Roman empire, the
wild beasts had long since retired from the face of man, and the neighbour-
hood of populous cities. To surprise them in their solitary haunts, and to
transport them to Rome, that they might be slain in pomp by the hand of
an emperor, was an enterprise equally ridiculous for the prince, and op-

pressive for the people. Ignorant of these distinctions, Commodus eagerly embraced the glorious resemblance, and styled himself (as we still read on his medals) the *Roman Hercules*. The club and the lion's hide were placed by the side of the throne, amongst the ensigns of sovereignty; and statues were erected, in which Commodus was represented in the character, and with the attributes, of the god. . . .

Elated with these praises, which gradually extinguished the innate sense of shame, Commodus resolved to exhibit, before the eyes of the Roman people, those exercises, which till then he had decently confined within the walls of his palace, and to the presence of a few favourites. On the appointed day, the various motives of flattery, fear, and curiosity, attracted to the amphitheatre an innumerable multitude of spectators; and some degree of applause was deservedly bestowed on the uncommon skill of the Imperial performer. Whether he aimed at the head or heart of the animal, the wound was alike certain and mortal. With arrows, whose point was shaped into the form of a crescent, Commodus often intercepted the rapid career, and cut asunder the long bony neck of the ostrich. A panther was let loose; and the archer waited until he had leaped upon a trembling malefactor. In the same instant the shaft flew, the beast dropt dead, and the man remained unhurt. The dens of the amphitheatre disgorged at once a hundred lions; a hundred darts from the unerring hand of Commodus laid them dead as they ran raging round the *Arena*. Neither the huge bulk of the elephant, nor the scaly hide of the rhinoceros, could defend them from his stroke. Ethiopia and India yielded their most extraordinary productions; and several animals were slain in the amphitheatre, which had been seen only in the representations of art, or perhaps of fancy. In all these exhibitions, the securest precautions were used to protect the person of the Roman Hercules from the desperate spring of any savage; who might possibly disregard the dignity of the emperor, and the sanctity of the god.

But the meanest of the populace were affected with shame and indignation when they beheld their sovereign enter the lists as a gladiator, and glory in a profession which the laws and manners of the Romans had branded with the justest note of infamy. He chose the habit and arms of the *Secutor*, whose combat with the *Retiarius* formed one of the most lively scenes in the bloody sports of the amphitheatre. The *Secutor* was armed with an helmet, sword, and buckler; his naked antagonist had only a large net and a trident; with the one he endeavoured to entangle, with the other to dispatch, his enemy. If he missed the first throw, he was obliged to fly from the pursuit of the *Secutor*, till he had prepared his net for a second cast. The emperor fought in this character seven hundred and thirty-five several times. These glorious achievements were carefully recorded in the public acts of the empire; and that he might omit no circumstance of infamy, he received from the common fund of gladiators, a stipend so exorbitant, that it became a new and most ignominious tax upon the Roman people. It may be easily supposed, that in these engagements the master of the world was always successful: in the amphitheatre his victories were not often sanguinary; but when he exercised his skill in the school of gladiators, or his own palace, his wretched antagonists were frequently honoured with a mortal wound from the hand of Commodus, and obliged to seal their flattery with their blood.

EDWARD GIBBON

The Decline and Fall of the Roman Empire, 1776–88

The first Christian believed to have been martyred in the Colosseum was Saint Ignatius of Antioch. The Roman Catholic Church celebrates his death on the first day of February each year, and tradition holds that Ignatius was a favored being who was personally blessed by Jesus. A nineteenth-century historian relates his final tragic moments.

Cited before Trajan . . . for his refusal to worship the gods, to that charge he [Saint Ignatius] answered by eloquently exposing the follies of Paganism. In the fear that the death of one so revered in the capital where he held sacred office might excite tumult, or reflect additional honour on the persecuted religion, he was ordered to be conducted to Rome, to suffer with malefactors in the amphitheatre. He heard that sentence with joy, assisted himself in fitting on his chains, and set out on foot for that long journey, like one travelling towards home.

Arrived here, he was consigned to the prefect of the City, and only respited till the recurrence of some festival, with the usual entertainments in the amphitheatre. Brought into this arena, he knelt, and exclaimed, in a loud voice, — "Romans present at this spectacle, know that I have not been brought to this place for any crime, but in order that by such means I may merit the fruition of the glory of God, for love of whom I have been made prisoner. I am the grain of His field, and must be ground by the teeth of the lions, that I may deserve to be converted into bread fit for His table."

The lions were then let loose, and instantly devoured him, leaving nothing of his body but the larger bones, which the Christians were able to collect, during the night, for interment.

Shortly after this event, A.D. 109, Trajan revoked the edict of persecution, and allowed the Christians to remain unmolested, though prohibited from the public exercise of their worship.

> **CHARLES ISADORE HEMANS**
> *The Story of Monuments*
> *in Rome and Her Environs,* 1864

Throughout the Romantic era, when Rome was an obligatory stop on the Grand Tour, many writers commented on the exquisite beauty of the Colosseum, especially by moonlight. One of the first to do so was the German poet Goethe, who visited the city toward the end of the eighteenth century.

THE COLOSSEUM BY MOONLIGHT

Of the beauty of a walk through Rome by moonlight it is impossible to form a conception, without having witnessed it. All single objects are swallowed up by the great masses of light and shade, and nothing but grand and general outlines present themselves to the eye. For three several days we have enjoyed to the full the brightest and most glorious nights. Peculiarly beautiful, at such a time, is the Coliseum. At night it is always closed. A hermit dwells in a little shrine within its range, and beggars of all kinds nestle beneath its crumbling arches: the latter had lit a fire on the arena, and a gentle wind bore down the smoke to the ground, so that the lower portion of the ruins was quite hid by it; while, above, the vast walls stood out in deeper darkness before the eye. As we stopped at the gate to contemplate the scene through the iron gratings, the moon shone brightly in the heavens above. Presently the smoke found its way up the sides, and through every chink and opening, while the moon lit it up like a cloud. The sight was exceedingly glorious. In such a light one ought also to see the Pantheon, the Capitol, the Portico of St. Peter's, and the grand streets and squares. And thus sun and moon, as well as the human mind, have here to do a work quite different from what they produce elsewhere, — here where vast and yet elegant masses present themselves to their rays.

JOHANN WOLFGANG VON GOETHE
Travels in Italy, France and Switzerland, 1787

The most famous and influential of the English Romantic poets was Lord Byron, whose verse-drama Manfred *took its inspiration directly from the Colosseum. Byron too passed many hours in the arena and found it beautiful by moonlight.*

When I was wandering, — upon such a night
I stood within the Coliseum's wall,
Midst the chief relics of almighty Rome;
The trees which grew along the broken arches
Waved dark in the blue midnight, and the stars
Shone through the rents of ruin; from afar
The watchdog bay'd beyond the Tiber; and
More near from out the Caesars' palace came
The owl's long cry, and, interruptedly,
Of distant sentinels the fitful song
Begun and died upon the gentle wind.
Some cypresses beyond the time-worn breach
Appear'd to skirt the horizon, yet they stood
Within a bowshot — Where the Caesars dwelt,
And dwell the tuneless birds of night, amidst
A grove which springs through levell's battlements,
And twines its roots with the imperial hearths,
Ivy usurps the laurel's place of growth; —
But the gladiators' bloody Circus stands,
A noble wreck in ruinous perfection!
While Caesar's chambers, and the Augustan halls,
Grovel on earth in indistinct decay. —
And thou didst shine, thou rolling moon, upon
All this, and cast a wide and tender light,
Which soften'd down the hoar austerity
Of rugged desolation, and fill'd up,
As 'twere anew, the gaps of centuries;
Leaving that beautiful which still was so,
And making that which was not, till the place
Became religion, and the heart ran o'er
With silent worship of the great of old! —
The dead, but sceptred sovereigns, who still rule
Our spirits from their urns. —

LORD BYRON
Manfred, 1817

The American poet and critic Edgar Allan Poe made one serious but incomplete attempt at drama. Entitled Politian, *it is set in Rome in the sixteenth century. Politian, the hero, soliloquizes in the interior of the Colosseum while awaiting the arrival of his lover, Lalage.*

Shall meet me here within the Coliseum!
Type of the antique Rome — rich reliquary
Of lofty contemplation left to Time
By buried centuries of pomp and power!
At length at length after so many days
Of weary pilgrimage, and burning thirst
 (Thirst for the springs of lore that in thee lie)
I stand, an altered and an humble man
Amid thy shadows, and so drink within
My very soul thy grandeur, gloom and glory!
She comes not, and the spirit of the place
Oppresses me!
Vastness and Age and Memories of Eld
Silence and Desolation and dim Night
Gaunt vestibules, and phantom-peopled aisles
I feel ye now — I feel ye in your strength!
O spells more sure than e'er Judaean king
Taught in the gardens of Gethsemane
O spells more potent than the rapt Chaldee
Ever drew down from out the quiet stars!
She comes not and the moon is high in Heaven!
Here where a hero fell, a column falls
Here where the mimic eagle glared in gold
A secret vigil holds the swarthy bat
Here where the dames of Rome their yellow hair
Waved to the wind, now wave the reed and thistle:
Here where on ivory couch the Caesar sate
On bed of moss lies gloating the foul adder:
Here where on golden throne the monarch lolled
Glides spectre-like unto his marble home
Lit by the wan light of the horned moon
The swift and silent lizard of the stones.
These crumbling walls — these tottering arcades
These mouldering plinths — these sad and blackened shafts
These vague entablatures: this broken frieze
These shattered cornices, this wreck, this ruin,
These stones, alas! these grey stones are they all
All of the great and the colossal left
By the corrosive hours to Fate and me?
Not all the echos answer me — not all:
Prophetic sounds and loud arise forever
From us and from all ruin unto the wise,
As from the granite Memnon to the sun.
We rule the hearts of mightiest men: we rule
With a despotic sway all giant minds.
We are not desolate we pallid stones,

Not all our power is gone — not all our Fame
Not all the magic of our high renown
Not all the wonder that encircles us
Not all the mysteries that in us lie
Not all the memories that hang upon
And cling around about us as a garment
Clothing us in a robe of more than glory.

EDGAR ALLAN POE
Politian: A Tragedy, 1833

The popular American landscape painter Thomas Cole was enchanted by almost everything he saw when he visited Rome in 1832. But it was the Colosseum — by moonlight — that stirred him most.

From the great multitude of wondrous things, I would select the Colosseum as the object that affected me the most. It is stupendous, yet beautiful in its destruction. . . . To walk beneath its crumbling walls, to climb its shattered steps, to wander through its long, arched passages, to tread in the footsteps of Rome's ancient kings, to muse upon its broken height, is to lapse into sad, though not unpleasing meditation.

But he who would see and feel the grandeur of the Colosseum must spend his hour there, at night, when the moon is shedding over it its magic splendour. Let him ascend to its higher terraces, at that pensive time, and gaze down into the abyss, or hang his eye upon the ruinous ridge, where it gleams in the moon-rays, and charges boldly against the deep blue heaven. The mighty spectacle, mysterious and dark, opens beneath the eye more like some awful dream than an earthly reality, — a vision of the valley and shadow of death, rather than the substantial work of man. Could man, indeed, have ministered either to its erection or its ruin? As I mused upon its great circumference, I seemed to be sounding the depths of some volcanic crater, whose fires, long extinguished, had left the ribbed and blasted rocks to the wildflower and the ivy. In a sense, the fancy is a truth: it was once the crater of human passions; there their terrible fires blazed forth with desolating power, and the thunder of the eruption shook the skies. But now all is still desolation. In the morning the warbling of birds makes the quiet air melodious; in the hushed and holy twilight, the low chanting of monkish solemnities soothes the startled ear.

THOMAS COLE
Notes at Naples, 1832

The English novelist Charles Dickens visited Rome in 1844. If he too saw the Colosseum by moonlight, he did not record his impressions; instead, in characteristic fashion, he registered a social rather than poetic reaction to the awesome monument.

It is no fiction, but plain, sober, honest Truth, to say: so suggestive and distinct is it [the "Coliseum"] at this hour: that, for a moment — actually in passing in — they who will, may have the whole great pile before them, as it used to be, with thousands of eager faces staring down into the arena, and such a whirl of strife, and blood, and dust, going on there, as no language can describe. Its solitude, its awful beauty, and its utter desolation, strike upon the stranger, the next moment, like a softened sorrow; and never in his life, perhaps, will he be so moved and overcome by any sight, not immediately connected with his own affections and afflictions.

To see it crumbling there, an inch a year; its walls and arches overgrown with green; its corridors open to the day; the long grass growing in its porches; young trees of yesterday, springing up on its ragged parapets, and bearing fruit: chance produce of the seeds dropped there by the birds who build their nests within its chinks and crannies; to see its Pit of Fight filled up with earth, and the peaceful Cross planted in the centre; to climb into its upper halls, and look down on ruin, ruin, ruin, all about it; the triumphal arches of Constantine, Septimius Severus [Emperor, A.D. 146–211], and Titus [Emperor, A.D. 79–81]; the Roman Forum; the Palace of the Caesars; the temples of the old religion, fallen down and gone; is to see the ghost of old Rome, wicked wonderful old city, haunting the very ground on which its people trod. It is the most impressive, the most stately, the most solemn, grand, majestic, mournful sight, conceivable. Never, in its bloodiest prime, can the sight of the gigantic Coliseum, full and running over with the lustiest life, have moved one heart, as it must move all who look upon it now, a ruin. GOD be thanked: a ruin!

As it tops the other ruins: standing there, a mountain among graves: so do its ancient influences outlive all other remnants of the old mythology and old butchery of Rome, in the nature of the fierce and cruel Roman people. The Italian face changes as the visitor approaches the city; its beauty becomes devilish; and there is scarcely one countenance in a hundred, among the common people in the streets, that would not be at home and happy in a renovated Coliseum to-morrow.

Here was Rome indeed at last; and such a Rome as no one can imagine in its full and awful grandeur! We wandered out upon the Appian Way, and then went on, through miles of ruined tombs and broken walls, with here and there a desolate and uninhabited house: past the Circus of Romulus, where the course of the chariots, the stations of the judges, competitors, and spectators, are yet as plainly to be seen as in old time: past the tomb of Cecilia Metella: past all inclosure, hedge, or stake, wall or fence: away upon the open Campagna, where on that side of Rome, nothing is to be beheld but Ruin. . . .

. . . by dint of going out early every morning, and coming back late every evening, and labouring hard all day, I believe we made acquaintance with every post and pillar in the city, and the country round; and, in particular, explored so many churches that I abandoned that part of the enterprise at last, before it was half finished, lest I should never, of my own accord, go to church again, as long as I lived. But, I managed, almost every day, at one time or other, to get back to the Coliseum, and out upon the open Campagna, beyond the Tomb of Cecilia Metella. . . .

And this reminds me that some Roman altars of peculiar sanctity, bear the inscription, "Every mass performed at this altar, frees a soul from Purgatory." I have never been able to find out the charge for one of these services, but they should needs be expensive. There are several Crosses in Rome too, the kissing of which, confers indulgences for varying terms. That in the centre of the Coliseum, is worth a hundred days; and people may be seen kissing it, from morning to night. It is curious that some of these crosses seem to acquire an arbitrary popularity; this very one among them. In another part of the

Coliseum there is a cross upon a marble slab, with the inscription, "Who kisses this cross shall be entitled to Two hundred and forty days' indulgence." But I saw no one person kiss it, though, day after day, I sat in the arena, and saw scores upon scores of peasants pass it, on their way to kiss the other. . . .

It is an awful thing to think of the enormous caverns that are entered from some Roman churches, and undermine the city. Many churches have crypts and subterranean chapels of great size, which, in the ancient time, were baths, and secret chambers of temples, and what not; but I do not speak of them. Beneath the church of St. Giovanni and St. Paolo, there are the jaws of a terrific range of caverns, hewn out of the rock, and said to have another outlet underneath the Coliseum — tremendous darknesses of vast extent, half-buried in the earth and unexplorable, where the dull torches, flashed by the attendants, glimmer down long ranges of distant vaults branching to the right and left, like streets in a city of the dead; and show the cold damp stealing down the walls, drip-drop, drip-drop, to join the pools of water that lie here and there, and never saw, and never will see, one ray of the sun. Some accounts make these the prisons of the wild beasts destined for the amphitheatre; some, the prisons of the condemned gladiators; some, both. But the legend most appalling to the fancy is, that in the upper range (for there are two stories of these caves) the Early Christians destined to be eaten at the Coliseum Shows, heard the wild beasts, hungry for them, roaring down below; until, upon the night and solitude of their captivity, there burst the sudden noon and life of the vast theatre crowded to the parapet, and of these, their dreaded neighbours, bounding in!

CHARLES DICKENS
Pictures from Italy, 1846

To the American writer Nathaniel Hawthorne the moon was too bright a light by which to view the Colosseum; the great amphitheater was made "too distinctly visible." He much preferred the dimness of starlight — and his own imagination.

Grassy as the lane was, it skirted along heaps of shapeless ruin, and the bare site of the vast temple that Hadrian [Emperor, A.D. 117–38] planned and built. It terminated on the edge of a somewhat abrupt descent, at the foot of which, with a muddy ditch between, rose, in the bright moonlight, the great curving wall and multitudinous arches of the Coliseum. . . .

. . . Within, the moonlight filled and flooded the great empty space; it glowed upon tier above tier of ruined, grass-grown arches, and made them even too distinctly visible. The splendor of the revelation took away that inestimable effect of dimness and mystery by which the imagination might be assisted to build a grander structure than the Coliseum, and to shatter it with a more picturesque decay. Byron's celebrated description is better than the reality. He beheld the scene in his mind's eye, through the witchery of many intervening years, and faintly illuminated it as if with starlight instead of this broad glow of moonshine.

. . . There was much pastime and gayety just then in the area of the Coliseum, where so many gladiators and wild beasts had fought and died, and where so much blood of Christian martyrs had been lapped up by that fiercest of wild beasts, the Roman populace of yore. Some youths and maidens were running merry races across the open space, and playing at hide-and-seek a little way within the duskiness of the ground-tier of arches, whence now and then you could hear the half-shriek, half-laugh of a frolicsome girl, whom the shadow had betrayed into a young man's arms. Elder groups were seated on the fragments of pillars and blocks of marble that lay round the verge of the arena, talking in the quick, short ripple of the Italian tongue. On the steps of the great black cross in the centre of the Coliseum sat a party singing scraps of songs, with much laughter and merriment between the stanzas.

It was a strange place for song and mirth. That black cross marks one of the special blood-spots of the earth where, thousands of times over, the dying gladiator fell, and more of human agony has been endured for the mere pastime of the multitude than on the breadth of many battle-fields. From all this crime and suffering, however, the spot has derived a more than common sanctity. An inscription promises seven years' indulgence, seven years of remission from the pains of purgatory, and earlier enjoyment of heavenly bliss, for each separate kiss imprinted on the black cross. What better use could be made of life, after middle-age, when the accumulated sins are many and the remaining temptations few, than to spend it all in kissing the black cross of the Coliseum!

Besides its central consecration, the whole area has been made sacred by a range of shrines, which are erected round the circle, each commemorating some scene or circumstance of the Savior's passion and suffering. In accordance with an ordinary custom a pilgrim was making his progress from shrine to shrine upon his knees, and saying a penitential prayer at each. Light-footed girls ran across the path along which he crept, or sported with their friends close by the shrines where he was kneeling. The pilgrim took no heed, and the girls meant no irreverence; for in Italy religion jostles along side by side with business and sport, after a fashion of its own, and people are accustomed to kneel down and pray, or see others praying, between two fits of merriment, or between two sins.

To make an end of our description, a red twinkle of light was visible amid the breadth of shadow that fell across the upper part of the Coliseum. Now it glimmered through a line of arches, or threw a broader gleam as it rose out of some profound abyss of ruin; now it was muffled by a heap of shrubbery which had adventurously clambered to that dizzy height; and so the red light kept ascending to loftier and loftier ranges of the structure, until it stood like a star where the blue sky rested against the Coliseum's topmost wall. It indicated a party of English or Americans paying the inevitable visit by moonlight, and exalting themselves with raptures that were Byron's, not their own.

Our company of artists, sat on the fallen column, the pagan altar, and the steps of the Christian shrine, enjoying the moonlight and shadow, the present gayety and the gloomy reminiscences of the scene, in almost equal share. Artists, indeed, are lifted by the ideality of their pursuits a little way off the earth. . . .

. . . "The Coliseum is far more delightful, as we enjoy it now, than when eighty thousand persons sat squeezed together, row above row, to see their fellow-creatures torn by lions and tigers limb from limb. What a strange thought that the Coliseum was really built for us, and has not come to its best uses till almost two thousand years after it was finished!"

NATHANIEL HAWTHORNE
The Marble Faun, 1859

In 1878 when Henry James wrote the novella Daisy Miller, *viewing the Colosseum by moonlight was very popular despite its supposed risks. One hazard, "Roman fever," was believed to be caused by excavators who had opened long-closed vaults in the arena and disturbed the ancient drainage system. James's heroine is a rich American girl traveling abroad for the first time. A fellow American named Winterbourne, who met the unsophisticated, yet flippant Daisy in Switzerland, has followed her to Rome — where she is already very much taken up with a handsome young Italian, named Giovanelli.*

Above was a moon half-developed, whose radiance was not brilliant but veiled in a thin cloud-curtain that seemed to diffuse and equalise it. When . . . at eleven o'clock he [Winterbourne] approached the dusky circle of the Colosseum the sense of the romantic in him easily suggested that the interior, in such an atmosphere, would well repay a glance. He turned aside and walked to one of the empty arches, near which, as he observed, an open carriage — one of the little Roman street-cabs — was stationed. Then he passed in among the cavernous shadows of the great structure and emerged upon the clear and silent arena. The place had never seemed to him more impressive. One half of the gigantic circus was in deep shade while the other slept in the luminous dusk. As he stood there he began to murmur Byron's famous lines out of "Manfred"; but before he had finished his quotation he remembered that if nocturnal meditation thereabouts was the fruit of a rich literary culture it was none the less deprecated by medical science. The air of other ages surrounded one; but the air of other ages, coldly analysed, was no better than a villainous miasma. Winterbourne sought, however, toward the middle of the arena, a further reach of vision, intending the next moment a hasty retreat. The great cross in the centre was almost obscured; only as he drew near did he make it out distinctly. He thus also distinguished two persons stationed on the low steps that formed its base. One of these was a woman seated; her companion hovered before her.

Presently the sound of the woman's voice came to him distinctly in the warm night-air. "Well, he [Winterbourne] looks at us as one of the old lions or tigers may have looked at the Christian martyrs!" These words were winged with their accent, so that they fluttered and settled about him in the darkness like vague white doves. It was Miss Daisy Miller who had released them for flight.

"Let us hope he's not very hungry" — the bland Giovanelli fell in with her humour. "He'll have to take *me* first; you'll serve for dessert."

Winterbourne felt himself pulled up with final horror now — and, it must be added, with final relief. It was as if a sudden clearance had taken place in the ambiguity of the poor girl's appearances and the whole riddle of her contradictions had grown easy to read. She was a young lady about the *shades* of whose perversity a foolish puzzled gentleman need no longer trouble his head or his heart. That once questionable quantity *had* no shades — it was a mere black little blot. He stood there looking at her, looking at her companion too, and not reflecting that though he saw them vaguely he himself must have been more brightly presented. He felt angry at all his shiftings of view — he felt ashamed of all his tender little scruples and all his witless little mercies. He was about to advance again, and then again checked himself; not from the fear of doing her injustice, but from a sense of the danger of showing undue exhilaration for this disburdenment of cautious criticism. He turned away toward the entrance of the place; but as he did so he heard Daisy speak again.

"Why it was Mr. Winterbourne! He saw me and he cuts me dead!"

What a clever little reprobate she was, he was amply able to reflect at this, and how smartly she feigned, how promptly she sought to play off on him, a surprised and injured innocence! But nothing would induce him to cut her either "dead" or to within any measurable distance even of the famous "inch" of her life. He came forward again and went toward the great cross. Daisy had got up and Giovanelli lifted his hat. Winterbourne had now begun to think simply of the madness, on the ground of exposure and infection, of a frail young creature's lounging away such hours in a nest of malaria. What if she *were* the most plausible of little reprobates? That was no reason for her dying of the *perniciosa*. "How long have you been 'fooling round' here?" he asked with conscious roughness.

Daisy, lovely in the sinister silver radiance, appraised him a moment, roughness and all. "Well, I guess all the evening." She answered with spirit and, he could see even then, with exaggeration. "I never saw anything so quaint."

"I'm afraid," he returned, "you'll not think a bad attack of Roman fever very quaint. This is the way people catch it. I wonder," he added to Giovanelli, "that you, a native Roman, should countenance such extraordinary rashness."

"Ah," said this seasoned subject, "for myself I have no fear."

"Neither have I — for you!" Winterbourne retorted in French. "I'm speaking for this young lady."

Giovanelli raised his well-shaped eyebrows and showed his shining teeth, but took his critic's rebuke with docility. "I assured Mademoiselle it was a grave indiscretion, but when was Mademoiselle ever prudent?"

"I never was sick, and I don't mean to be!" Mademoiselle declared. "I don't look like much, but I'm healthy! I was bound to see the Colosseum by moonlight — I wouldn't have wanted to go home without *that*; and we've had the most beautiful time, haven't we, Mr. Giovanelli? If there has been any danger Eugenio can give me some pills. Eugenio has got some splendid pills."

"*I* should advise you then," said Winterbourne, "to drive home as fast as possible and take one!"

Giovanelli smiled as for the striking happy thought. "What you say is very wise. I'll go and make sure the carriage is at hand." And he went forward rapidly.

Daisy followed with Winterbourne. He tried to deny himself the small fine anguish of looking at her, but his eyes themselves refused to spare him, and she seemed moreover not in the least embarrassed. He spoke no word; Daisy chattered over the beauty of the place: "Well, I *have* seen the Colosseum by moonlight — that's one thing I can rave about!" Then noticing her companion's silence she asked him why he was so stiff — it had always been her great word. He made no answer, but he felt his laugh an immense negation of stiffness. They passed under one of the dark archways; Giovanelli was in front with the carriage. Here Daisy stopped a moment, looking at her compatriot. "*Did* you believe I was engaged the other day?"

"It doesn't matter now what I believed the other day!" he replied with infinite point.

It was a wonder how she didn't wince for it. "Well, what do you believe now?"

"I believe it makes very little difference whether you're engaged or not!"

He felt her lighted eyes fairly penetrate the thick gloom of the vaulted passage — as if to seek some access to him she hadn't yet compassed. But Giovanelli, with a graceful inconsequence, was at present all for retreat. "Quick, quick; if we get in by midnight we're quite safe!"

Daisy took her seat in the carriage and the fortunate Italian placed himself beside her. "Don't forget Eugenio's pills!" said Winterbourne as he lifted his hat.

"I don't care," she unexpectedly cried out for this, "whether I have Roman fever or not!" On which the cab-driver cracked his whip and they rolled across the desultory patches of antique pavement.

Winterbourne — to do him justice, as it were — mentioned to no one that he had encountered Miss Miller at midnight in the Colosseum with a gentleman; in spite of which deep discretion, however, the fact of the scandalous adventure was known a couple of days later, with a dozen vivid details, to every member of the little American circle, and was commented accordingly. Winterbourne judged thus that the people about the hotel had been thoroughly empowered to testify, and that after Daisy's return there would have been an exchange of jokes between the porter and the cab-driver. But the young man became aware at the same moment of how thoroughly it had ceased to ruffle him that the little American flirt should be "talked about" by low-minded menials. These sources of current criticism a day or two later abounded still further: the little American flirt was alarmingly ill and the doctors now in possession of the scene. Winterbourne, when the rumour came to him, immediately went to the hotel for more news. . . .

. . . It was clear that Daisy was dangerously ill.

Winterbourne constantly attended for news from the sick-room, which reached him, however, but with worrying indirectness, though he once had speech, for a moment, of the poor girl's physician. . . .

. . . A week after this the poor girl died; it had been indeed a terrible case of the *perniciosa*. A grave was found for her in the little Protestant cemetery, by an angle of the wall of imperial Rome, beneath the cypresses and the thick spring-flowers. Winterbourne stood there beside it with a number of other mourners; a number larger than the scandal excited by the young lady's career might have made probable.

HENRY JAMES
Daisy Miller, 1878

A BOTANIST'S DELIGHT

In 1855, the English botanist Richard Deakin carefully cataloged the different species of plants growing in the Colosseum — and discovered an astonishing 420 varieties. The book he published on the subject is a painstaking, beautifully illustrated record of the array of flowers that once scattered gay colors across the monumental ruin.

The object of the present little volume is to call the attention of the lover of the works of creation to those floral productions which flourish, in triumph, upon the ruins of a single building. Flowers are perhaps the most graceful and lovely objects of the creation but are not, at any time, more delightful than when associated with what recalls to the memory time and place, and especially that of generations long passed away. They form a link in the memory, and teach us hopeful and soothing lessons, amid the sadness of bygone ages: and cold indeed must be the heart that does not respond to their silent appeal; for though without speech, they tell of that regenerating power which reanimates the dust of mouldering greatness, and clothes their sad and fallen grandeur with graceful forms and curiously constructed leaves and flowers, resplendent with their gay and various colours, and perfume the air with their exquisite odours.

The plants which we have found growing upon the Colosseum, and have here described, amount to no less a number than 420 species; in this number there are examples of 253 Genera, and illustrations of 66 of the Natural Orders of plants, a number which seems almost incredible. There are 56 species of Grasses — 47 of the order *Compositoe* or Syngenesious plants — and 41 of the Leguminous or Pea tribe: but it must be remembered that, though the ground occupied by the building is about six acres, the surface of the walls and lodgment on the ruins upon which they grow is much more extensive, and the variety of soil is much greater, than would be supposed without examination; for, on the lower north side, it is damp, and favourable to the production of many plants, while the upper walls and accumulated mould are warmer and dryer, and, consequently, better suited for the development of others: and, on the south side, it is hot and dry, and suited only for the growth of differently constructed tribes.

The collection of the plants and the species noted has been made some years; but since that time, many of the plants have been destroyed, from the alterations and restorations that have been made in the ruins; a circumstance that cannot but be lamented. To preserve a further falling of any portion is most desirable; but to carry the restorations, and the brushing and cleaning, to the extent to which it has been subjected, instead of leaving it in its wild and solemn grandeur, is to destroy the impression and solitary lesson which so magnificent a ruin is calculated to make upon the mind. . . .

[A description of individual plants follows, beginning with the anemone.] This extremely beautiful early spring flower is very generally distributed in shady places in all parts of the South of Europe; it varies in colour, from a pale pink, to a deep rose colour, according to the more or less exposed situation in which it grows. . . . It grows in various parts of the Colosseum, and there flowers freely, glowing in its bright colours like a joyous star upon the mouldering remains of past generations.

This pretty little plant [dianthus, which includes Old World pinks and carnations] grows very abundantly on the lower ruins around the arena of the Colosseum; frequently it is a very small plant in dry, exposed situations, arising probably from the want of moisture. It is generally distributed throughout Europe, in sterile places, road-sides, etc.

. . . Perhaps there are few persons who will notice this plant [paliurus or Christ's Thorn] flourishing upon the vast ruins of the Colosseum of Rome, without being moved to reflect upon the scenes that have taken place on the spot on which he stands, and remember the numbers of those holy men who bore witness to the truth of their belief in Jesus, and shed their blood before the thousands of Pagans assembled around, as a testimony, securing for themselves an eternal crown, without thorns, and to us those blessed truths, on which only we build our future hope of bliss, and derive our present peace and comfort.

RICHARD DEAKIN
Flora of the Colosseum, 1855

Henry Wadsworth Longfellow used the flora of the Colosseum as an imagistic device in his verse-drama Michael Angelo. *In this dialogue from the work, the Renaissance painter ignores the amphitheater's bloody past and presents the arena as an object as beautiful as a rose.*

CAVALIERI   What do you here alone, Messer Michele?
MICHAEL ANGELO   I come to learn.
CAVALIERI   You are already master,
And teach all other men.
MICHAEL ANGELO   Nay, I know nothing;
Not even my own ignorance, as some
Philosopher hath said. I am a school-boy
Who hath not learned his lesson, and who stands
Ashamed and silent in the awful presence
Of the great master of antiquity
Who built these walls cyclopean.
CAVALIERI   Gaudentius
His name was, I remember. His reward
Was to be thrown alive to the wild beasts
Here where we now are standing.
MICHAEL ANGELO   Idle tales.
CAVALIERI   But you are greater than Gaudentius was,
And your work nobler.
MICHAEL ANGELO   Silence, I beseech you.
CAVALIERI   Tradition says that fifteen thousand men
Were toiling for ten years incessantly
Upon this amphitheatre.
MICHAEL ANGELO   Behold
How wonderful it is! The queen of flowers
The marble rose of Rome! Its petals torn
By wind and rain of thrice five hundred years;
Its mossy sheath half rent away, and sold
To ornament our palaces and churches,
Or to be trodden under feet of man
Upon the Tiber's bank; yet what remains
Still opening its fair bosom to the sun,
And to the constellations that at night
Hang poised above it like a swarm of bees.
CAVALIERI   The rose of Rome, but not of Paradise;
Not the white rose our Tuscan poet saw,
With saints for petals. When this rose was perfect
Its hundred thousand petals were not saints,
But senators in their Thessalian caps,
And all the roaring populace of Rome;
And even an Empress and the vestal Virgins,
Who came to see the gladiators die,
Could not give sweetness to a rose like this.
MICHAEL ANGELO   I spake not of its uses, but its beauty.
CAVALIERI   The sand beneath our feet is saturate
With blood of martyrs; and these rifted stones
Are awful witnesses against a people

Whose pleasure was the pain of dying men.

MICHAEL ANGELO Tomaso Cavalieri, on my word,
You should have been a preacher, not a painter!
Think you that I approve such cruelties,
Because I marvel at the architects
Who built these walls, and curved these noble arches?
Oh, I am put to shame, when I consider
How mean our work is, when compared with theirs!
Look at these walls about us and above us!
They have been shaken by earthquakes, have been made
A fortress, and been battered by long sieges;
The iron clamps, that held the stone together,
Have been wrenched from them; but they stand erect
And firm, as if they had been hewn and hollowed
Out of the solid rock, and were a part
Of the foundations of the world itself.

CAVALIERI Your work, I say again, is nobler work,
In so far as its end and aim are nobler;
And this is but a ruin, like the rest.
Its vaulted passages are made the caverns
Of robbers, and are haunted by the ghosts
Of murdered men.

MICHAEL ANGELO A thousand wild flowers bloom
From every chink, and the birds build their nests
Among the ruined arches, and suggest
New thoughts of beauty to the architect.
Now let us climb the broken stairs that lead
Into the corridors above, and study
The marvel and the mystery of that art
In which I am a pupil, not a master.
All things must have an end; the world itself
Must have an end, as in a dream I saw it.
There came a great hand out of heaven, and touched
The earth, and stopped it in its course.
The seas
Leaped, a vast cataract, into the abyss; . . .

CAVALIERI But the earth does not move.

MICHAEL ANGELO Who knows? who knows?
There are great truths that pitch their shining tents
Outside our walls, and though but dimly seen
In the gray dawn, they will be manifest
When the light widens into perfect day.
A certain man, Copernicus by name,
Sometime professor here in Rome, has whispered
It is the earth, and not the sun, that moves.
What I beheld was only in a dream,
Yet dreams sometimes anticipate events,
Being unsubstantial images of things
As yet unseen.

HENRY WADSWORTH LONGFELLOW
Michael Angelo, 1869

154

ANDROCLES
AND THE LION

The Colosseum has also been an inspiration to twentieth-century writers. In 1912, the brilliant dramatist George Bernard Shaw used it as a setting for his mock-heroic play Androcles and the Lion. *The work is based on the legendary tale of a first-century Christian who befriends a lion that ultimately saves his life. Following are excerpts from the two-act burlesque with the author's eccentricities of spelling (most notably his disdain of apostrophes in contractions) preserved intact. The action begins with Androcles and his wife, Megaera, quarreling in a lion-infested jungle.*

ANDROCLES (*whispering*)   Did you see? A lion.

MEGAERA (*despairing*)   The gods have sent him to punish us because you're a Christian. Take me away, Andy. Save me.

ANDROCLES (*rising*)   Meggy: theres one chance for you. Itll take him pretty nigh twenty minutes to eat me. (I'm rather stringy and tough) and you can escape in less time than that.

MEGAERA   Oh, dont talk about eating. (*The lion rises with a great groan and limps towards them*). Oh! (*She faints*).

ANDROCLES (*quaking, but keeping between the lion and Megaera*)   Dont you come near my wife, do you hear? (*The lion groans. Androcles can hardly stand for trembling*). Meggy: run. Run for your life. If I take my eye off him, it's all up. (*The lion holds up his wounded paw and flaps it piteously before Androcles*). Oh, he's lame, poor old chap! He's got a thorn in his paw. A frightfully big thorn. (*Full of sympathy*) Oh, poor old man! Did um get an awful thorn into um's tootsums wootsums? Has it made um too sick to eat a nice little Christian man for um's breakfast? Oh, a nice little Christian man will get um's thorn out for um; and then um shall eat the nice Christian man and the nice Christian man's nice big tender wifey pifey. (*The lion responds by moans of self-pity*). Yes, yes, yes, yes, yes. Now, now (*taking the paw in his hand*), um is not to bite and not to scratch, not even if it hurts a very very little. Now make velvet paws. Thats right. (*He pulls gingerly at the thorn. The lion, with an angry yell of pain, jerks back his paw so abruptly that Androcles is thrown on his back*). Steadeee! Oh, did the nasty cruel little Christian man hurt the sore paw? (*The lion moans assentingly but apologetically*). Well, one more little pull and it will be all over. Just one little, little, leetle pull; and then um will live happily ever after. (*He gives the thorn another pull. The lion roars and snaps his jaws with a terrifying clash*). Oh, mustnt frighten um's good kind doctor, um's affectionate nursey. That didnt hurt at all: not a bit. Just one more. Just to shew how the brave big lion can bear pain, not like the little crybaby Christian man. Oopsh! (*The thorn comes out. The lion yells with pain, and shakes his paw wildly*). Thats it! (*Holding up the thorn*). Now it's out. Now lick um's paw to take away the nasty inflammation. See? (*He licks his own hand. The lion nods intelligently and licks his paw industriously*). Clever little liony-piony! Understands um's dear old friend Andy Wandy. (*The lion licks his face*). Yes, kissums Andy Wandy. (*The lion, wagging his tail violently, rises on his hind legs, and embraces Androcles, who makes a wry face and cries*) Velvet paws! Velvet paws! (*The lion draws in his claws*). Thats right. (*He embraces the lion, who finally takes the end of his tail in one paw, places that tight round Androcles' waist, resting it on his hip. Androcles takes the other paw in his hand, stretches out his arm, and the two waltz rapturously round and round and finally away through the jungle*).

After helping the lion, Androcles is captured by the Romans and taken to the Colosseum, where he waits with a group of fellow Christians to die in the arena. Among Androcles's companions are Lavinia, a beautiful, resolute young woman; Spintho, a cowardly debauchee; Ferrovius, a huge Christian with a gladiator's instincts and also Lavinia's brother; and the Editor, superintendent of public games.

LAVINIA Will they [the gladiators] really kill one another?

SPINTHO Yes, if the people turn down their thumbs.

THE EDITOR You know nothing about it. The people indeed! Do you suppose we would kill a man worth perhaps fifty talents to please the riffraff? I should like to catch any of my men at it.

SPINTHO I thought —

THE EDITOR (*contemptuously*) You thought! Who cares what you think? Youll be killed all right enough.

SPINTHO (*groans and again hides his face*) !!!

LAVINIA Then is nobody ever killed except us poor Christians?

THE EDITOR If the vestal virgins turn down their thumbs, thats another matter. Theyre ladies of rank.

LAVINIA Does the Emperor ever interfere?

THE EDITOR Oh, yes: he turns his thumbs up fast enough if the vestal virgins want to have one of his pet fighting men killed.

ANDROCLES But dont they ever just only pretend to kill one another? Why shouldnt you pretend to die, and get dragged out as if you were dead; and then get up and go home, like an actor?

THE EDITOR See here: you want to know too much. There will be no pretending about the new lion: let that be enough for you. Hes hungry.

SPINTHO (*groaning with horror*) Oh, Lord! cant you stop talking about it? Isnt it bad enough for us without that?

ANDROCLES I'm glad hes hungry. Not that I want him to suffer, poor chap! but then hell enjoy eating me so much more. Theres a cheerful side to everything.

THE EDITOR (*rising and striding over to Androcles*) Here: dont you be obstinate. Come with me and drop the pinch of incense on the altar. Thats all you need do to be let off.

ANDROCLES No: thank you very much indeed; but I really mustnt.

THE EDITOR What! Not to save your life?

ANDROCLES Id rather not. I couldnt sacrifice to Diana: shes a huntress, you know, and kills things.

THE EDITOR That dont matter. You can choose your own altar. Sacrifice to Jupiter: he likes animals: he turns himself into an animal when he goes off duty.

ANDROCLES No: its very kind of you; but I feel I cant save myself that way.

THE EDITOR But I dont ask you to do it to save yourself: I ask you to do it to oblige me personally.

ANDROCLES (*scrambling up in the greatest agitation*) Oh, please dont say that. That is dreadful. You mean so kindly by me that it seems quite horrible to disoblige you. If you could arrange for me to sacrifice when theres nobody looking, I shouldnt mind. But I must go into the arena with the rest. My honor, you know.

THE EDITOR Honor! The honor of a tailor?

156

ANDROCLES (*apologetically*)   Well, perhaps honor is too strong an expression. Still, you know, I couldnt allow the tailors to get a bad name through me.

THE EDITOR   How much will you remember of all that when you smell the beast's breath and see his jaws opening to tear out your throat?

SPINTHO (*rising with a yell of terror*)   I cant bear it. Wheres the altar? I'll sacrifice.

FERROVIUS   Dog of an apostate. Iscariot!

SPINTHO   I'll repent afterwards. I fully mean to die in the arena: I'll die a martyr and go to heaven; but not this time, not now, not until my nerves are better. Besides, I'm too young: I want to have just one more good time. (*The gladiators laugh at him*). Oh, will no one tell me where the altar is? (*He dashes into the passage and vanishes*).

ANDROCLES (*to the Editor, pointing after Spintho*)   Brother: I cant do that, not even to oblige you. Dont ask me.

THE EDITOR   Well, if youre determined to die, I cant help you. But I wouldnt be put off by a swine like that.

FERROVIUS   Peace, peace: tempt him not. Get thee behind him, Satan.

THE EDITOR (*flushing with rage*)   For two pins Id take a turn in the arena myself to-day, and pay you out for daring to talk to me like that.

Ferrovius springs forward.

LAVINIA (*rising quickly and interposing*)   Brother, brother: you forget.

FERROVIUS (*curbing himself by a mighty effort*)   Oh, my temper, my wicked temper! (*To the Editor, as Lavinia sits down again, reassured*). Forgive me, brother. My heart was full of wrath: I should have been thinking of your dear precious soul.

THE EDITOR   Yah! (*He turns his back on Ferrovius contemptuously, and goes back to his seat*).

FERROVIUS (*continuing*)   And I forgot it all: I thought of nothing but offering to fight you with one hand tied behind me.

THE EDITOR (*turning pugnaciously*)   What!

FERROVIUS (*on the border line between zeal and ferocity*)   Oh, dont give way to pride and wrath, brother. I could do it so easily. I could —

They are separated by the Menagerie Keeper, who rushes in from the passage, furious.

THE KEEPER   Heres a nice business! Who let that Christian out of here down to the dens when we were changing the lion into the cage next the arena?

THE EDITOR   Nobody let him. He let himself.

THE KEEPER   Well, the lion's ate him. . . . Now his appetite's taken off, he wont as much as look at another Christian for a week.

> *Awaiting her turn in the arena, Lavinia converses with a handsome young captain in the Praetorian Guard. The captain has been saying that martyrdom is senseless, that both her Christianity and his paganism are fairy tales. Lavinia counters that one must have something to die for in order to make life worth living. Meanwhile, Ferrovius has been thrust into the arena, where, no longer able to be a good Christian and turn the other cheek, he chooses to fight for his life.*

FERROVIUS   Lost! lost forever! I have betrayed my Master. Cut off this right hand: it has offended. Ye have swords, my brethren: strike.

LAVINIA   No, no. What have you done, Ferrovius?

157

FERROVIUS   I know not; but there was blood behind my eyes; and theres blood on my sword. What does that mean?

THE EMPEROR (*enthusiastically, on the landing outside his box*)   What does it mean? It means that you are the greatest man in Rome. It means that you shall have a laurel crown of gold. Superb fighter, I could almost yield you my throne. It is a record for my reign: I shall live in history. Once, in Domitian's time, a Gaul slew three men in the arena and gained his freedom. But when before has one naked man slain six armed men of the bravest and best? The persecution shall cease: if Christians can fight like this, I shall have none but Christians to fight for me. (*To the Gladiators*) You are ordered to become Christians, you there: do you hear?

RETIARIUS   It is all one to us, Caesar. Had I been there with my net, the story would have been different.

THE CAPTAIN (*suddenly seizing Lavinia by the wrist and dragging her up the steps to the Emperor*)   Caesar: this woman is the sister of Ferrovius. If she is thrown to the lions he will fret. He will lose weight; get out of condition —

THE EMPEROR   The lions? Nonsense! (*To Lavinia*) Madam: I am proud to have the honor of making your acquaintance. Your brother is the glory of Rome.

LAVINIA   But my friends here. Must they die?

THE EMPEROR   Die! Certainly not. There has never been the slightest idea of harming them. Ladies and gentlemen: you are all free. Pray go into the front of the house and enjoy the spectacle to which your brother has so splendidly contributed. Captain: oblige me by conducting them to the seats reserved for my personal friends.

THE MENAGERIE KEEPER   Caesar: I must have one Christian for the lion. The people have been promised it; and they will tear the decorations to bits if they are disappointed.

THE EMPEROR   True, true: we must have somebody for the new lion.

FERROVIUS   Throw me to him. Let the apostate perish.

THE EMPEROR   No, no: you would tear him in pieces, my friend; and we cannot afford to throw away lions as if they were mere slaves. But we must have somebody. This is really extremely awkward.

THE MENAGERIE KEEPER   Why not that little Greek chap? Hes not a Christian: hes a sorcerer.

THE EMPEROR   The very thing: he will do very well.

THE CALL BOY (*issuing from the passage*)   Number twelve. The Christian for the new lion.

ANDROCLES (*rising, and pulling himself sadly together*)   Well, it was to be, after all.

LAVINIA   I'll go in his place Caesar. Ask the Captain whether they do not like best to see a woman torn to pieces. He told me so yesterday.

THE EMPEROR   There is something in that: there is certainly something in that — if only I could feel sure that your brother would not fret.

ANDROCLES   No: I should never have another happy hour. No: on the faith of a Christian and the honor of a tailor, I accept the lot that has fallen on me. If my wife turns up, give her my love and say that my wish was that she should be happy with her next, poor fellow! Caesar: go to your box and see how a tailor can die. Make way for number twelve there. (*He marches out . . .*).

  The vast audience in the amphitheatre now sees the Emperor re-enter his box and take his place as Androcles, desperately frightened, but still march-

ing with piteous devotion, emerges from the other end of the passage, and finds himself at the focus of thousands of eager eyes. The lion's cage, with a heavy portcullis grating, is on his left. The Emperor gives a signal. A gong sounds. Androcles shivers at the sound; then falls on his knees and prays. The grating rises with a clash. The lion bounds into the arena. He rushes round frisking in his freedom. He sees Androcles. He stops; rises stiffly by straightening his legs; stretches out his nose forward and his tail in a horizontal line behind, like a pointer, and utters an appalling roar. Androcles crouches and hides his face in his hands. The lion gathers himself for a spring, swishing his tail to and fro through the dust in an ecstasy of anticipation. Androcles throws up his hands in supplication to heaven. The lion checks at the sight of Androcles's face. He then steals towards him; smells him; arches his back; purrs like a motor car; finally rubs himself against Androcles, knocking him over. Androcles, supporting himself on his wrist, looks affrightedly at the lion. The lion limps on three paws, holding up the other as if it was wounded. A flash of recognition lights up the face of Androcles. He flaps his hand as if it had a thorn in it, and pretends to pull the thorn out and to hurt himself. The lion nods repeatedly. Androcles holds out his hands to the lion, who gives him both paws, which he shakes with enthusiasm. They embrace rapturously, finally waltz round the arena amid a sudden burst of deafening applause, and out through the passage, the Emperor watching them in breathless astonishment until they disappear, when he rushes from his box and descends the steps in frantic excitement.

THE EMPEROR   My friends, an incredible! an amazing thing! has happened. I can no longer doubt the truth of Christianity. (*The Christians press to him joyfully*) This Christian sorcerer — (*with a yell, he breaks off as he sees Androcles and the lion emerge from the passage waltzing. He bolts wildly up the steps into his box, and slams the door. All, Christians and gladiators alike, fly for their lives, the gladiators bolting into the arena, the others in all directions. The place is emptied with magical suddenness*).

ANDROCLES (*naively*)   Now I wonder why they all run away from us like that. (*The lion combining a series of yawns, purrs, and roars, achieves something very like a laugh*).

THE EMPEROR (*standing on a chair inside his box and looking over the wall*) Sorcerer: I command you to put that lion to death instantly. It is guilty of high treason. Your conduct is most disgra — (*the lion charges at him up the stairs*) help! (*He disappears. The lion rears against the box; looks over the partition at him, and roars. The Emperor darts out through the door and down to Androcles, pursued by the lion*).

ANDROCLES   Dont run away, sir: he cant help springing if you run. (*He seizes the Emperor and gets between him and the lion, who stops at once*). Dont be afraid of him.

THE EMPEROR   I am not afraid of him. (*The lion crouches, growling. The Emperor clutches Androcles*) Keep between us.

ANDROCLES   Never be afraid of animals, your Worship: thats the great secret. He'll be as gentle as a lamb when he knows that you are his friend. Stand quite still; and smile; and let him smell you all over just to reassure him; for, you see, hes afraid of you; and he must examine you thoroughly before he gives you his confidence. (*To the lion*) Come now, Tommy; and speak nicely to the Emperor, the great, good Emperor who has power to have all our heads cut off if we dont behave very, very respectfully to him.

The lion utters a fearful roar. The Emperor dashes madly up the steps, across the landing, and down again on the other side, with the lion in hot pursuit. Androcles rushes after the lion; overtakes him as he is descending; and throws himself on his back, trying to use his toes as a brake. Before he can stop him the lion gets hold of the trailing end of the Emperor's robe. . . .

ANDROCLES   We mustnt let him lash himself into a rage. You must shew him that you are my particular friend — if you will have the condescension. (*He seizes the Emperor's hands and shakes them cordially*). Look, Tommy: the nice Emperor is the dearest friend Andy Wandy has in the whole world: he loves him like a brother.

THE EMPEROR   You little brute, you damned filthy little dog of a Greek tailor: I'll have you burnt alive for daring to touch the divine person of the Emperor. (*The lion growls*).

ANDROCLES   Oh dont talk like that, sir. He understands every word you say: all animals do: they take it from the tone of your voice. (*The lion growls and lashes his tail*). I think hes going to spring at your worship. If you wouldnt mind saying something affectionate. (*The lion roars*).

THE EMPEROR   (*shaking Androcles' hands frantically*)   My dearest Mr. Androcles, my sweetest friend, my long lost brother, come to my arms. (*He embraces Androcles*). Oh, what an abominable smell of garlic!

The lion lets go the robe and rolls over on his back, clasping his forepaws over one another coquettishly above his nose.

ANDROCLES   There! You see, your worship, a child might play with him now. See! (*He tickles the lion's belly. The lion wriggles ecstatically*). Come and pet him.

THE EMPEROR   I must conquer these unkingly terrors. Mind you dont go away from him, though. (*He pats the lion's chest*).

ANDROCLES   Oh, sir, how few men would have the courage to do that!

THE EMPEROR   Yes: it takes a bit of nerve. Let us have the Court in and frighten them. Is he safe, do you think?

ANDROCLES   Quite safe now, sir.

THE EMPEROR   (*majestically*)   What ho, there! All who are within hearing, return without fear. Caesar has tamed the lion. . . . And now, my friends, though I do not, as you see, fear this lion, yet the strain of his presence is considerable; for none of us can feel quite sure what he will do next.

THE MENAGERIE KEEPER   Caesar: give us this Greek sorcerer to be a slave in the menagerie. He has a way with the beasts.

ANDROCLES (*distressed*)   Not if they are in cages. They should not be kept in cages. They must all be let out.

THE EMPEROR   I give this sorcerer to be a slave to the first man who lays hands on him. (*The menagerie keepers and the gladiators rush for Androcles. The lion starts up and faces them. They surge back*). You see how magnanimous we Romans are, Androcles. We suffer you to go in peace.

ANDROCLES   I thank your worship. I thank you all, ladies and gentlemen. Come, Tommy. Whilst we stand together, no cage for you: no slavery for me. (*He goes out with the lion, everybody crowding away to give him as wide a berth as possible*).

GEORGE BERNARD SHAW
Androcles and the Lion, 1912

REFERENCE

Chronology of Roman History

Entries in boldface refer to the Colosseum.

B.C. 753	Traditional date of the founding of Rome by Romulus		253	**Sempronius, Olympius, Theodolus, and Exuperia burned alive before statue of the sun-god at arena's entrance**
509	Traditional date Roman Republic founded		284	Diocletian proclaimed emperor
105	First official gladiatorial contest		c. 293	Empire divided for easier administration
71	Spartacus's revolt crushed		**303–13**	**Great persecution of Christians**
44	Julius Caesar assassinated		306	Constantine proclaimed coemperor
31	Octavian defeats Antony at Actium		312	Constantine wins the battle of Milvian Bridge and becomes sole ruler
27	Augustus proclaimed first emperor; *Pax Romana* — 200 years of peace — begins		**320**	**Colosseum struck by lightning**
			324	Constantine reunites empire
A.D. 54	Nero proclaimed emperor		330	Constantine dedicates Constantinople as capital of his empire; Christianity becomes the official religion
64	Fire destroys Rome; first persecution of Christians			
68	Nero commits suicide		**354**	**Last mention of the colossal statue of Nero that gave arena its name**
69	Vespasian, founder of Flavian dynasty, proclaimed emperor		392	Pagan worship prohibited
70	Titus besieges Jerusalem		395	Roman Empire permanently divided into West and East (Byzantine Empire)
72	**Construction of arena begins**		397–401	Saint Augustine writes *The Confessions*
79	Death of Vespasian; Titus proclaimed emperor; Mount Vesuvius erupts		**404–5**	**Saint Telemachus martyred; Honorius abolishes gladiatorial games**
80	**Colosseum dedicated by Titus; arena subject of a book by the Roman poet Martial**		410	Alaric sacks Rome
			422	**Colosseum damaged by earthquake**
80	Fire ravages Rome		455	Vandals sack Rome
81	Death of Titus; Domitian proclaimed emperor		476	Last emperor, Romulus Augustulus, deposed by Odoacer; traditional date of collapse of Western Roman Empire
81–96	**Construction of arena completed**		**508**	**Colosseum damaged by earthquake**
96	Assassination of Domitian, last of the Flavian emperors		**523**	**Last recorded animal games held**
c. 110	**First recorded martyrdom in the arena, that of Saint Ignatius of Antioch**		535–54	Byzantines recapture Italy; Ravenna becomes capital of Western Empire
180	Commodus proclaimed emperor		**c. 730**	**Arena first called the "Colosseum" by the Venerable Bede**
200	**Women gladiators banned from arena**		800	Charlemagne crowned at St. Peter's, ending Byzantine rule
c. 230	**Restoration by Alexander Severus**			
248	**One-thousandth anniversary of Rome celebrated in the arena**		846	Saracens raid outskirts of Rome
249	Decius institutes violent persecution of Christians		847	**Earthquake damages Colosseum**

914–63	Nadir of papacy; Rome rent by rivalry among ruling families
1084	Normans under Robert Guiscard plunder Rome
1144	**Arena converted into a stronghold by its owners, the Frangipani family**
1167	Frederick Barbarossa conquers Rome
1231	**Earthquake damages Colosseum**
1244	**Annibaldi family acquires half ownership from Frangipanis**
1255	**Arena damaged by earthquake**
1263	**Religious plays staged in the arena**
1312	**Presented to city of Rome by the Holy Roman Emperor Henry VII**
1332	**Bullfighting tournament held**
1349	**Damaged by earthquake**
1362	**Pope Urban V auctions stones**
c. 1400	**Used as a quarry in construction of palaces, mansions, other structures**
1451–52	**2,522 cartloads of stone removed to construct Vatican and Roman walls**
1471–1549	Period of great Renaissance popes
1490	**First Passion play performed**
1522	**Bull said to have been sacrificed to appease devils during plague**
1527	Charles de Bourbon sacks Rome
1534	**Religious plays abolished**
1558–62	Benvenuto Cellini writes *Autobiography*
1585–90	**Conversion into wool factory proposed by Pope Sixtus V**
1626	New St. Peter's Basilica consecrated
1675	**Arena becomes dumping ground in the manufacture of gunpowder**
1703	**Damaged by earthquake**
1725	**Proposal made to add baroque church**
1744	**Dedicated to Christian martyrs by Pope Benedict XIV; Stations of Cross erected; destruction ceases**

1776–88	Edward Gibbon writes *The Decline and Fall of the Roman Empire*
1798	French under Napoleon occupy Rome and declare Italy a republic
1809	Papal States annexed to France
1812	**First weeding by French**
c. 1815	**Restoration begun by Pope Pius VII**
1817	Byron composes *Manfred*
1825	**Pope Leo XII adds supporting buttress**
1832	**Proposal to convert into city cemetery**
1848	**Used for political orations**
1849	Garibaldi defeated by French troops; revolutionary movement suppressed
1852	**Second weeding by French; restoration by Pope Pius IX**
1852–59	Ministry of Count Cavour
1855	**Deakin publishes *Flora of the Colosseum***
1860	**Further restoration by Pope Pius IX**
1861	Kingdom of Italy proclaimed, with Victor Emmanuel as first monarch
1870	Rome becomes capital of Italy
1871	**All plants removed by Romans**
1893–96	**Nearby buildings removed; interior structures laid bare**
1922	Mussolini comes to power
1929	Lateran Treaties restore temporal power of papacy over Vatican City
1933	**Mussolini builds boulevard, Via dei Fori Imperiali, freeing Colosseum from nearby structures**
1940	Italy enters World War II
1944	Rome falls to Allies
1948	**Postwar tourist boom begins**
1951	**Concert performed in arena on anniversary of Verdi's death**
1960	Olympics held at Rome
1962–65	Second Vatican Council

Guide to Roman Monuments

Symbol of Rome's eternity and perhaps the most famous ruin in the world, the Colosseum was known in antiquity as the Flavian Amphitheater, after the three emperors of that dynasty who had a hand in its construction. Vespasian conceived the idea of building the arena, and construction began in A.D. 72. His son Titus dedicated the amphitheater in A.D. 80 with an inaugural festival that lasted one hundred days and included bloody gladiatorial contests, fights with wild beasts, and full-scale naval battles for which the arena was flooded. Construction was completed during the reign of Vespasian's younger son, Domitian (A.D. 81–96). It probably acquired its present name from the colossal statue of Nero — itself a wonder — which stood nearby.

Like the pyramids in Egypt, the Colosseum is a marvel both of architecture and engineering. The outer framework and the skeleton of the interior up to the second story were built of huge travertine blocks; softer stones and concrete completed the structure. The interior was faced with precious marbles, looted centuries ago. Columns of the Doric, Ionic, and Corinthian orders completely girdled the structure, and an enormous awning could be hoisted to protect the audience in the event of rain.

A mammoth mass of stone, the Colosseum enclosed elliptically one-third of a mile, measured 620 feet by 513 feet, sprawled across 6 acres, had 3 tiers of seats, soared 4 stories into the air, and possessed 80 entrances to give 45,000 to 50,000 balky spectators plenty of elbow room. Its statistics resemble those of the Astrodome Stadium at Houston, Texas, built in 1965, which is 710 feet in diameter and seats 45,000.

WITHIN THE ETERNAL CITY

THE PANTHEON

The best preserved of ancient Rome's monuments and the most famous after the Colosseum is the Pantheon. Its name, which honors Rome's many planetary deities, is still more commonly used than Santa Maria ad Martyres, acquired in A.D. 608 when it was consecrated as a Christian church by Pope Boniface IV. The temple was built in 27 B.C. by the statesman and general Marcus Agrippa, but owes its present appearance to Hadrian, who restored it between A.D. 115 and 124. So perfectly proportioned that its architecture was imitated in buildings all over the ancient world, the Pantheon's most striking features are its monumental portico supported by sixteen granite columns, its original great bronze doors, and a vast concrete dome roofing the rotunda. An opening in the center of the dome, twenty-eight feet in diameter, is its only source of light. Its brick exterior remains much as it always was, but over the centuries its interior has been altered. The great Renaissance painter Raphael was buried there, as were several Italian kings, beginning with the newly united nation's first monarch, Victor Emmanuel II.

THE THEATER OF MARCELLUS

Begun by Julius Caesar and completed by Augustus in A.D. 13, the Theater of Marcellus bears the name of Augustus's favorite nephew, who died at the age of twenty-five. Used as a music hall by the ancients, it was probably the architectural inspiration for the Colosseum. Like the arena, its half-columns on the arcades are Doric at ground level, Ionic on the first story, and Corinthian on the second. After Rome fell, it was used as a quarry — as was the Colosseum. It became a fortress in the twelfth century, a palace in the sixteenth, and at present part of it is an apartment house.

THE ROMAN FORUM

To the untrained eye it may appear to be no more than a ruin-studded park, but to archaeologists and other students of ancient history the Roman Forum evokes visions of the glory of Rome at its height. Its arches, columns, crumbling walls, and scattered stones — covering several acres between the Capitol and the Palatine Hill — recall major events in the history of the ancient Roman state from the republican period (509–31 B.C.), when it was the political, religious, and commercial center of Roman life, through the sumptuous, often decadent imperial era (31 B.C.–A.D. 476).

The Roman Forum's most important ruins include:
- The Lapis Niger, or black stone, laid down, it was said, over the tomb of Romulus, legendary founder of Rome in the eighth century B.C.
- The Temple of Saturn, founded in 498 B.C., one of the most venerated monuments of republican Rome. It was the scene of a licentious annual festival called the Saturnalia.
- The Temple of Castor and Pollux, built in 484 B.C. in honor of the military exploits of two mythical heroes who came to be identified with the constellation Gemini.
- The Temple of Concord, erected in 367 B.C. to commemorate the resolution of a bitter political breach between the Senate and people of Rome.
- The *rostra* or platforms, where tribunes and consuls delivered their most famous orations.
- The Basilica Aemilia, first built in 179 B.C., beautified in 78 B.C., later reconstructed by Augustus, and nearly destroyed in A.D. 410 when the Gothic leader Alaric sacked Rome.
- The Mamertine Prison, the state prison of ancient Rome, where Jugurtha and Vercingetorix, who waged wars against Rome in the first century B.C., were tortured and died.
- The Curia, where the Senate met; improved by Julius Caesar and Diocletian.
- The Basilica Julia, begun by Julius Caesar and finished by Augustus, where civil cases were tried.
- The Temple of Julius Caesar, erected in 29 B.C. on the site of Caesar's cremation fifteen years earlier.
- The Arch of Augustus, built in 29 B.C. to celebrate Augustus's victory over

Antony and Cleopatra in the decisive battle of Actium.
- The Temple of Vespasian, erected in honor of the emperor who conceived the idea of the Colosseum.
- The Arch of Titus, one of Rome's most famous monuments, constructed during Domitian's reign to commemorate the victories of Titus and Vespasian in the Judaean War, which ended with the sack of Jerusalem in A.D. 70. A relief depicts the triumphal procession bearing the spoils of the Temple of Jerusalem. Another relief shows the apotheosis of Titus, who is carried to heaven by an eagle.
- The House and Temple of the Vestals, built in the first century A.D., where six holy virgins lived and tended a sacred fire that was believed to have been brought to Rome from Troy by the legendary hero Aeneas.

- The Basilica of Constantine or Maxentius, the Forum's largest monument and one of the most impressive remaining examples of Roman architecture. Begun in A.D. 306 by Maxentius and completed soon after by Constantine, it is said to have inspired Michelangelo's design for the dome of St. Peter's.

- The Regia, the traditional residence of Numa Pompilius and subsequently the official palace of the Pontifex Maximus, the priest in charge of the Vestals.
- The Temple of Antoninus and Faustina, dedicated first to the emperor's wife in A.D. 141 and then also to the emperor himself in A.D. 161; converted into a Christian church and given a baroque façade in 1602.
- The Arch of Septimius Severus, erected in A.D. 213 in honor of the emperor and his two sons, Caracalla and Geta, to commemorate their many military victories.
- The Temple of Romulus, built in the fourth century A.D., known for its splendid bronze doors.
- Santa Maria Antiqua, the Forum's oldest Christian building. Originally constructed by Domitian, it may have become a church as early as the sixth century A.D.
- Column of Phocas, the last addition to the Forum, built in A.D. 608 by Smaragdus, Exarch of Italy, to honor the centurian Phocas, who seized Byzantium in 602 and thereby became emperor of the Eastern Roman Empire.

THE IMPERIAL FORUMS
Between 54 B.C. and A.D. 113, five other forums were built in Rome to supplement the old Forum, which was no longer large enough to serve the city's many foreign visitors and burgeoning population.
- The Forum of Julius Caesar, built in the decade immediately preceding his assassination in 44 B.C.
- The Forum of Augustus, with the Temple of Mars Ultor commemorating the battle of Philippi in 42 B.C.

- The Forum of Vespasian, with the Temple of Peace, erected with the spoils of the Judaean campaign.
- The Forum of Nerva, erected between A.D. 90 and 97.
- The Forum of Trajan, built in A.D. 114, the largest and most splendid of the imperial forums. All that remains is part of a basilica and Trajan's Column, the most conspicuous monument of the five forums. The column is 108 feet high (including a statue of Saint Peter at the summit that replaced one of Trajan in 1587). Winding around the column is a spiral frieze of bas-reliefs that realistically depicts some 2,500 soldiers engaged in the Dacian campaigns in Central Europe.

In addition to the forums, many other ancient wonders dot the Eternal City:

THE APPIAN WAY
The famous road, constructed in 312 B.C., passes the Circus of Maxentius, the tomb of Cecilia Metella, the superb gate of San Sebastiano, an outstanding Roman aqueduct, and the world-famous catacombs—subterranean burial grounds of ancient Jews and Christians.

THE ARCH OF CONSTANTINE
Erected almost in the Colosseum's shadow, this arch is covered with reliefs depicting scenes from the lives of Constantine, Trajan, and Marcus Aurelius.

THE BATHS OF CARACALLA
These surpass in luxury and splendor all the other baths of ancient Rome. There, 1,600 bathers could take hot, cold, or tepid baths, enjoy a massage, converse, stroll, read, or play games. In modern times, operas have been staged in the great ruin, one of the largest outdoor theaters in the world.

THE BATHS OF DIOCLETIAN
The largest baths of ancient Rome, they cover an area of more than a million square feet.

THE TEMPLE OF FORTUNA VIRILIS
Built about 100 B.C., this temple may be incorrectly named because it is not known to which gods it was dedicated.

THE COLUMN OF MARCUS AURELIUS
Ninety-eight feet tall, its reliefs show the second-century emperor's victories over the Germans.

THE PYRAMID OF GAIUS CESTIUS
Rome's only pyramid towers sixty feet over the Protestant Cemetery, where the nineteenth-century English poets Keats and Shelley are buried.

THE CASTRO PRETORIO
Once the headquarters of the crack imperial household troop, the Praetorian Guard, this building is now called the Caserma del Macao, and was until recently a military barrack.

CASTEL SANT'ANGELO
This building was begun by Hadrian in A.D. 135 as the imperial tomb for himself and his successors. In the Middle Ages it was fortified and connected to the Vatican by an elevated passage that could be used as an escape route by the pope in time of danger.

THE AURELIAN WALL
Built in A.D. 271–75, it completely surrounds the ancient part of the city.

OUTSIDE THE ETERNAL CITY

The Romans were not only great builders in their capital, Rome, but also throughout a vast empire, which at its height in the first and second centuries A.D. stretched all the way from Britain to Mesopotamia.

Devoted to the sports of human and animal combat, the Romans constructed amphitheaters in many parts of their world. One of the largest after the Colosseum was built in the first century A.D. in Verona. It is 430 feet wide by

500 feet long, and held roughly 25,000 spectators. Theatrical performances are still performed in the arena. Other important amphitheaters were erected at Naples, Pompeii, Pozzuoli, and Pola in Italy, and at Arles and Nîmes in France.

One of the best-preserved examples of a Roman temple is known as the Maison Carrée, or Square House, at

Nîmes. Among other examples outside Rome are the Temple of Minerva at Assisi, those at Pompeii, and the Temple of Vesta at Tivoli. In the Middle East are the temples of Bacchus and Venus at Baalbek, and of the Sun at Palmyra. One dedicated to Augustus was built on the Acropolis at Athens.

The most luxurious of the imperial palaces was Hadrian's villa at Tivoli,

which was begun about A.D. 123. It was embellished with fountains, statues, pools, lakes, canals, avenues of cypresses, and full-scale reproductions of the most interesting buildings Hadrian had seen on his travels. The palace of Diocletian at Split in Yugoslavia is another great example of Roman imperial building.

The best-preserved Roman theater is the one at Orange, France. Others are located at Taormina in Sicily; Pompeii and Ostia in Italy; Termessus, Alinda, Aizani, and Aspendus in Asia Minor; and at Athens.

Arches commemorating the military exploits of various emperors were erected throughout the empire: at Benevento and Ancona in Italy, Orange and Nîmes in France, Pola in Yugoslavia, Susa in Iran, Tebessa and Timgad in Algeria, and Maktar in Tunisia.

One of the most famous and best-preserved Roman city gates is the Porta Nigra at Trier in Germany; the most

familiar Roman aqueducts are the several in the countryside around Rome, the Pont du Gard at Nîmes, and those at Segovia and Tarragona in Spain.

Entire cities were erected by the Romans all over Italy, then throughout the empire — from England to Romania and from Germany to North Africa.

When Hadrian visited Roman Britain in A.D. 122, he conceived the idea of building a great Roman fortification. The result was the celebrated Hadrian's Wall, which wound across the high moors between England and Scotland 73.5 miles from Wallsend-on-Tyne to Bowness-on-Solway, with forts and turrets continuing down the Cumberland coast to Moresby. Like the Berlin Wall dividing East and West Germany in modern times, Hadrian's Wall was an expression of military panic, for Hadrian greatly feared the fierce Scottish tribesmen who lived beyond the farthest northern reach of the ancient Roman world.

Selected Bibliography

Brown, Frank E. *Roman Architecture*. New York: George Braziller, 1961.

Cellini, Benvenuto. *The Life of Benvenuto Cellini*. Translated by John Addington Symonds. London: Macmillan Ltd., 1920.

Gibbon, Edward. *The History of the Decline and Fall of the Roman Empire*. Abridgment by D. M. Low. New York: Harcourt, Brace and World, 1966.

Goethe, Johann Wolfgang von. *Italian Journey*. Translated by W. H. Auden and Elizabeth Mayer. New York: Pantheon Books, 1962.

Grant, Michael. *The Climax of Rome*. London: Weidenfield & Nicolson, Ltd., 1968.

Grant, Michael. *The Gladiators*. New York: Delacorte Press, 1967.

Gregorovius, Ferdinand. *The Roman Journals of Ferdinand Gregorovius*. Edited by Friedrich Althous, translated by Gustavus W. Hamilton. London: G. Bell & Son, Ltd., 1911.

Hanfmann, George M. A. *Roman Art: A Modern Survey of the Art of Imperial Rome*. New York: New York Graphic Society, 1964.

Hibbert, Christopher. *The Grand Tour*. New York: G. P. Putnam's Sons, 1969.

Payne, Robert. *Ancient Rome*. New York: American Heritage Publishing Co., Inc., 1966.

Perowne, Stewart. *The End of the Roman World*. London: Hodder & Stoughton, Ltd., 1966.

Quennell, Peter. *Byron in Italy*. New York: The Viking Press, Inc., 1941.

Scherer, Margaret R. *Marvels of Ancient Rome*. London: Phaidon Press Ltd., 1955.

Suetonius. *The Twelve Caesars*. Translated by Robert Graves. London: The Folio Society, 1957.

Tacitus. *The Annals (Tacitus on Imperial Rome)*. Translated by Michael Grant. London: Penguin Books Ltd., 1956.

Tacitus. *The Histories*. Translated by Kenneth Wellesley. London: Penguin Books Ltd., 1964.

Acknowledgments and Picture Credits

The Editors would like to express their particular appreciation to James MaHood for his assistance in compiling The Colosseum in Literature and the Reference sections on pages 139-67, and to Kate Lewin in Paris and Josephine Powell in Rome for their assistance in obtaining pictorial material.

Peter Quennell and the Editors make grateful acknowledgment for the use of excerpted material from the following works:

Androcles and the Lion by George Bernard Shaw. Copyright 1930 by George Bernard Shaw. The excerpts appearing on pages 155-60 are reproduced by permission of the Society of Authors.

The Annals (Tacitus on Imperial Rome) by Tacitus. Translated by Michael Grant. Copyright 1956 by Michael Grant. The excerpts appearing on pages 48 and 61 are reproduced by permission of Penguin Books Ltd.

De Spectaculis by Tertullian. Translated by T. R. Glover. The excerpt appearing on page 75 is reproduced by permission of THE LOEB CLASSICAL LIBRARY and the publishers, Cambridge, Mass.: Harvard University Press.

Epigrams by Martial. Translated by Walter C. A. Ker. The excerpts describing the Colosseum and gladiatorial combat on page 139 are reproduced by permission of THE LOEB CLASSICAL LIBRARY and the publishers, Cambridge, Mass.: Harvard University Press.

Epistulae Morales (Epistles) by Seneca. Translated by Richard M. Gummere. The description of the brutality of gladiatorial combat on pages 59-60 is reproduced by permission of THE LOEB CLASSICAL LIBRARY and the publishers, Cambridge, Mass.: Harvard University Press.

Garibaldi's Defence of the Roman Republic by G. M. Trevelyan. The excerpt appearing on page 127 is reproduced by permission of Longmans Green and Company.

The Histories by Tacitus. Translated by Kenneth Wellesley. Copyright 1964 by Kenneth Wellesley. The excerpts appearing on page 22 are reproduced by permission of Penguin Books Ltd.

The title or description of each picture appears after the page number (boldface), followed by its location. Photographic credits appear in parentheses.

ENDPAPERS Model of Rome, *c.* A.D. 350. Circus Maximus, lower left, Colosseum, upper right. Museo della Civiltà Romana, Rome (Gabinetto Fotografico Nazionale, Rome)   HALF TITLE Symbol designed by Jay J. Smith Studio   FRONTISPIECE Head of Roman copy of Hellenistic bronze wrestler, *c.* 2nd century B.C. Museo Nazionale, Rome (Josephine Powell)   **10** Onyx relief of Roman eagle, late 1st century B.C. Kunsthistorisches Museum, Vienna   **12** Head of statue of Titus, *c.* 1st century A.D. Museo Nazionale, Naples (Anderson)

CHAPTER I   **17** top, Obverse of coin of Nero, A.D. 66-67. American Numismatic Society (Geoffrey Clements)   **17** bottom, The Golden House of Nero (Federico Arborio Mella, Milan)   **20** Portrait bust of Vespasian. Museo Capitolino, Rome (Pasquale De Antonis)   **22** Detail from the Arch of Titus, 1st century A.D. (Alinari)   **24-25** Fresco of the marriage of Venus and Mars. House of Marcus Lucretius, Pompeii (Fabrizio Parisio)   **26** Statue of Titus, 1st century A.D. Museo Nazionale, Naples (Anderson)   **28** Detail of Vespasian and Domitian from the Cancelleria Reliefs, 1st century A.D. Vatican (Pasquale De Antonis)   **29** Obverse of aureus of Domitia, A.D. 81-84. American Numismatic Society (Geoffrey Clements)   **30** Detail from the Column of Trajan, A.D. 114 (Fototeca Unione, Rome)   **32-33** (Josephine Powell)

CHAPTER II   **36** Reverse of *sestertius* of Titus, A.D. 80-81 (Josephine Powell)   **37** (Josephine Powell)   **38** Elevation and cross section of Colosseum from Luigi Canina, *Gli Edifizii di Roma Antica,* 1851 (Contessa Pecci Blunt, Josephine Powell)   **39** Elevation and cross section of Colosseum from Carlo Fontana, *L'Anfiteatro Flavio,* 1725 ed. (New York Public Library)   **40** (Josephine Powell)   **42-43** (Josephine Powell)   **44** Bronze figurine of Roman gladiator. Bibliothèque Nationale, Paris   **46** Fresco of Vulcan's workshop, Pompeii. National Archaeological Museum, Naples (Josephine Powell)   **47** Bronze gladiator's helmet, Pompeii. Museo Nazionale, Naples (Alinari)   **49** Fresco of brawl between Pompeians and Nucerians, Pompeii, A.D. 59. National Archaeological Museum, Naples (Josephine Powell)   **50** Frieze of gladiators fighting six bears, from Colosseum (Josephine Powell)   **52** Fresco of a comic scene from house of P. Casca Longus. Pompeii (Josephine Powell)   **53** Reverse of Trajan's coin of the Circus Maximus, A.D. 104-11. American Numismatic Society (Geoffrey Clements)   **55** Terracotta relief of a racing chariot, 1st century A.D. Townley Collection, British Museum (Michael Holford)

CHAPTER III   **58** Catacomb of St. Calixtus (Erich Lessing, Magnum)   **59** Mosaic of Christ as the sun-god from the Mausoleum of the Julii. Vatican (Pasquale De Antonis)   **60** Terracotta relief of gladiators fighting lions and a bear. Museo Teatrale alla Scala, Milan   **63** Manuscript illumination of the martyrdom of St. Ignatius from the *Menologium of Basil II,* 976-1025. Vatican Library, Ms. Greco, 1613, fol. 258   **64** Portrait bust of Commodus, 2nd century A.D. Museo dei Conservatori, Rome (Alinari)   **65** Detail from an arch of Marcus Aurelius. Museo Capitolino, Rome (Anderson)   **67** Mosaic of gladiators. Villa Borghese, Rome (Pasquale De Antonis)   **69** Relief of taxpayers, 3rd century A.D. Landesmuseum, Trier   **70** Manuscript illumination of Constantine, 9th century A.D. Bibliothèque Nationale, Paris, Ms. Grec, 510

Index

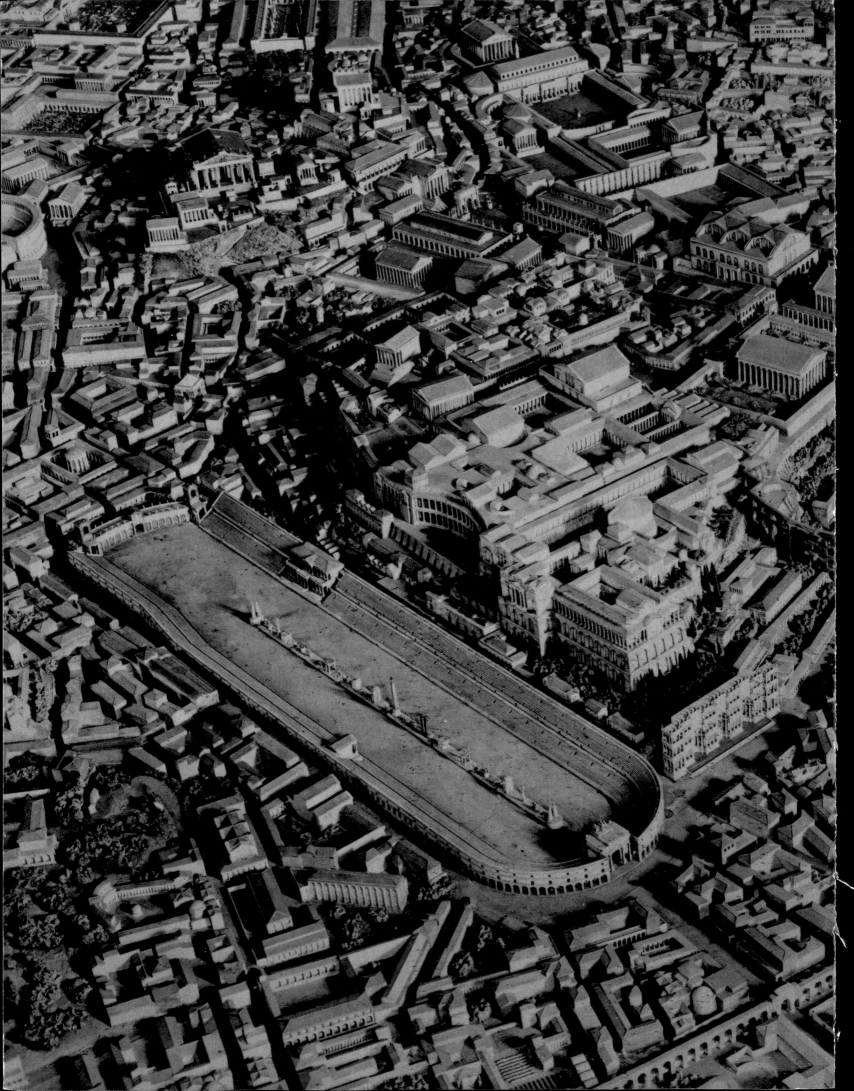